Rosemary Hart

Judith Tucci

Lois Boykin

Virginia Boehme

Part One

Portfolio

Corporate Leaders

This book has been made possible by the generous support of the sponsors listed below, support which has added immeasurably to the charitable work of the Montrose Garden Club.

FIRST NATIONAL BANK OF
BALDWIN COUNTY

Grand Hotel
POINT CLEAR RESORT & SPA
Marriott.

Montrose Garden Club

Jacket illustration by Louise Estes

ISBN 0-9741374-7-2

Published by American Image Publishing in cooperation with the Montrose Garden Club.

© 2008 American Image Publishing. All rights reserved. First edition published November 2008

Montrose Garden Club

PO Box 583

Montrose, AL 36559

Every effort has been made to ensure the accuracy of the information contained in this book.

However, the authors and publisher are not responsible for any errors or omissions that may have occurred.

Manufactured in South Korea

Acknowledgements

We wish to thank the many people who have helped to make this book possible. We appreciate the cooperation, enthusiasm, and encouragement that was given us as we made this journey. We have met so many interesting people and made many new friends. This has truly been a community supported book that would have not been possible without the corporate and retail sponsors, patrons and plant lovers.

We truly appreciate the owners of gardens, private and public, that allowed us to photograph their wonderful plants. We regret we could not use all the hundreds plus pictures we took. Thanks for your kindness: Robert Berglin, Paul and Karen Myrick, Van and Wanda Crocker, Thomas and Michelle Ollinger, James E. and Peggy Hasser, Sally Lieberman Clark, Jane McLendon, Inman and Linda Ellis, Philip and Mary Flo Williams, Valerie Faddis, Mike and Rosemary Hart, Elizabeth Rockwell, Jack and Lois Boykin, Mike and Judy Lucci, Art & Marilyn Holder, Drs. Fabien and Nicole Eyal, Jerry Mosley, Harris and Fran Morrisette, Dr. Adrian Bodet, Bobby and Debbie Green, Judy Thompson, Barry and Stevie Gaston, Conrad and Gigi Armbrecht, Charles Erwin, Clay Adams, Paul Fontenot, Leon Saltz, Peter Sikorowski, R.L. Smith, Rebecca Trosclair, Ben Carpenter, Bill Barrick at Bellingrath Gardens, Marion Drummond at the Mobile Botancial Gardens, City of Foley, Antique Rose Gardens, and the Marriott Grand Hotel at Point Clear. Please accept our apology if we have failed to mention a fellow gardener.

We owe a special thanks to artist, Louise Estes, for the lovely cover and illustrations of the perennials, annuals and vegetables. We are so very indebted to Fred Nation for the many hours he has spent proofing our work, giving us his expert advice as well as taking the time to write several articles.

A special thanks to the many artists who allowed us to use their work. We regret we did not have room for every piece of work offered.

And finally, to Jim Turner, Publisher, and Joe O'Donnell, Editor, you have become our treasured life time friends. Without you, *In Full Bloom* and *Live Oaks and Gentle Folks* would never have become reality. The Montrose Garden Club and our live oak trees will always be indebted to you.

Book Committee

Lois A. Boykin

Valerie Faddis

Rosemary Hart

Judy Lucci

Elizabeth Rockwell

Bea Sheldon

Table of Contents

Introduction

The Beauty of Growing Things

Published by the Montrose Garden Club, this book features colorful art, photographs and informative essays about gardens, gardening and the plants that brighten the lives of visitors and residents of Mobile and Baldwin Counties.

Plant and gardening experts from all over the region have contributed their tips, expertise and stories. Local artists and photographers have captured the beauty of the area's gardens with colorful portfolios that make *In Full Bloom* both informative and entertaining.

On the pages that follow, you will find a deep and abiding appreciation for the beauty that grows from the soil surrounding Mobile Bay.

This book has been divided into three distinct parts: Portfolio, Bloom and Resources. Each of these parts is designed to offer readers a glimpse at the beauty of growing things.

In Portfolio, you'll find essays and images that capture four distinct areas of the Mobile Bay region: the delta, the bog, the beach, and the bay. In each of these ecological areas, you'll find valuable and evocative insights into the unique attributes of the flora, climate and experience.

In the Bloom section, you'll find chapters that offer tips, information, and beautiful images that capture the beauty and majesty of everything from roses to ornamental grasses to camellias.

The Resources section offers a complete dossier of the plant life chronicled in this book, as well as information about soil testing and an appreciation of the sponsors and retailers who are making the distribution of this book possible.

We hope you'll enjoy this experience of life on Mobile Bay as depicted *In Full Bloom*.

A sunflower welcomes a new day. Photo by Kim Pearson

The Mobile-Tensaw Delta

A Reverie

by Fred Nation

Portfolio

The Delta is a rich tapestry of sunny marshes, dark brooding swamps, and quiet, lovely backwaters.

Somewhere in the Mobile-Tensaw Delta; 4 a.m.

When the tide changes near daylight the fall fishing should be good. The running lights and compass cast eerie red, green and blue halos in the dense October bay-fog. I cannot see the bow of the boat, the water, the trees, or the creatures of the night that I am certain can see and hear me. As I creep along there are muffled swirls and splashes, but I am unable to judge their distance or direction. Mullet are jumping somewhere nearby. My mind is certainly focused, but I am not exactly frightened by the fog and the darkness and the splashes. Not exactly.

Twenty miles or so above here the waters of two great rivers, the Alabama and the Tombigbee, join and flow together for a few miles, before separating again to form the second-largest river delta in the United States. As if they dislike flowing together, they quickly transform themselves into a wondrous tapestry of dozens and then hundreds of slews, channels, cutoff lakes, bayous, creeks, swamps and marshes. To be sure, there is land here, but the land of the delta is wet and subservient, owing its tentative existence to the water, continuously altered by the ebb and flow of the ever-present water. The rich alluvial land in the delta supports miles of magnificent forests and some of the largest trees in Alabama. On the north bank

The Delta is a tapestry of habitats: grassy marshes are interwoven with dark swamps and miles of creeks and sloughs. Photo by Stephen Savage

of Jessamine Bayou, west of Stockton, stands a water hickory that is 135 feet tall, with a trunk that is more than 12 feet in circumference. Nearby, in the alluvial swamp, a monstrous old baldcypress stands 131 feet tall, with a girth of more than 27 feet. These two giant trees are state champions, the largest of their kind known to exist in Alabama.

The Mobile-Tensaw Delta is about 35 miles long, from north-to-south, and 6 to 10 miles wide, depending on where it is measured. The southern limit is traditionally considered to be the Causeway, as locals refer to the highway that has connected the Eastern Shore to the Mobile Side since the 1920s. This location, on the north end of Mobile Bay, is important to understanding the rich bounty of the

delta. The bay is of the ocean, and it brings tides and salty water to the marshes, swamps and channels. The big rivers to the north deliver an astonishing average flow on the order of 60,000 cubic feet of fresh water per second to the delta and eventually to Mobile Bay.

Transition zones, where salt and fresh waters mix, where rivers meet the sea, are called estuaries, and they are among the most diverse and productive habitats on this earth. During dry times, and most years in the fall, the warm, turbid waters of the delta clarify to a rich green color, and they become brackish. Blue crabs are common on the shallow bottoms, and barnacles begin to grow on the trees, as creatures of the bay teem northward to feed and breed in the nutrient-rich swamps and marshes of the delta.

Common Reed, Phragmites australis on the Causeway.

Swamps and marshes are very different things. Swamps are dark and shady, with tupelo, red maple, baldcypress, sweetbay and ash trees towering above dark, still waters. Marshes are sunny, often with exposed, wet ground, and they are dominated by herbaceous plants. Some of our most beautiful native wildflowers are marsh plants: lovely purple pickerel weeds, stunning red cardinal flowers, marsh hibiscus, blue flag iris, and pure white swamp lilies are all frequently seen in our delta marshes. Many of these famous marsh plants are cultivated and sold in garden centers and plant sales.

Some places have an aura, a special feeling about them. One such place is Mound Island, on Bottle Creek, in the heart of the delta. There, 700 years ago, the Mississippians, one of the most advanced pre-European cultures in North America, flourished. They built at least 18 earthen mounds for their homes and temples. The largest of these is an astonishing 45 feet high. Archaeologists tell us that by 1500 the mound builders were mysteriously gone. A strange, formal feeling comes when one stands on that ancient ceremonial site, thinking of the people who lived and loved there, who built their houses, made their beautiful pottery, raised their children, worshipped their gods, and are no more. We can feel their presence in that sad, quiet place, and sometimes I think I can hear their spirits as they whisper to each other among the soaring trees.

I relax a bit when the pale yellow glow of dawn appears low in the eastern sky. As the fog clears into a beautiful fall morning, I decide

Below: Pickerelweed, Pontederia cordata, has become popular in backyard ponds and constructed wetlands. At right: Saltmarsh Mallow, Kosteletzkya virginica. Flowers are bright pink jewels in delta marshes during the summer and fall.

not to fish. I have my cameras, and I spend the day slowly cruising and drifting along the tree-lined sloughs and channels in the center of the delta. Along the muddy, sunny banks there are hundreds of arrowhead plants, which were collected as a staple by the mound-builders and later Indians for their starchy, nutritious roots. American Lotus is magnificent along the largest waterways, with ten-inch creamy white flowers that mature into strange fruits that look like inverted shower-heads. Fumbling with the camera, I miss a terrific

photograph of a great blue heron that flies by on slow-beating wings, with its body reflected on the still water. I take a passable photo of a ten-foot alligator as it climbs out of the water after warily eying me for several minutes.

My reveries are banished by the low growl of late afternoon thunder and a gray metallic sky to the north. The delta is no place to be during a thunderstorm with lightning, so I head back to the Causeway and to safety. To my right as I head home, I see the Mobile

skyline, with its bridges and great buildings. To my left, the high bluffs of Baldwin County rise out of the banks of the Blakeley River. I wonder how many of those thousands of people on both sides of the delta are aware of the incomparable treasure they have in their midst, just a few miles from their doorsteps.

Today, as I pen these lines and recall that perfect fall day in the delta, my thoughts drift into the distant shores of the future. I hope the majestic Mobile-Tensaw Delta will always be here; that the dreamers and idlers of tomorrow will share my delight in majestic blue herons, stunning wildflowers, and the splashes of mullet in the creepy darkness. My hope for those kindred spirits is that they will always have big trees as their cathedrals and the quiet solitude of dark delta waters to restore their souls.

Generations of coastal gardeners have planted and loved Southern Blue Flag Iris, *Iris virginica*.

Biography: Fred Nation

Fred Nation is a field botanist, freelance writer and photographer who lives in Daphne, Al. He teaches environmental subjects and "Plant Nomenclature" for the Baldwin and Mobile County Master Gardener intern classes, and for the Adult Learning Center in Fairhope. Fred conducts regular classes on habitats and ecosystems for the Volunteers at Weeks Bay Reserve. He has constructed interpreted nature trails for the City of Daphne, Blakeley State Park, Turtle Point Environmental Science Center (in Escambia County), and Camp Beckwith.

Fred has made many presentations for workshops and seminars for the USDA Forest Service, The Alabama Cooperative Extension System, and Weeks Bay Reserve.

He is on the Board of Directors of Blakeley State Park and Mobile Botanical Gardens, and he is a member of the Baldwin County Environmental Advisory Board.

Fred has nominated or co-nominated 21 Alabama State Champion Trees in Baldwin County, and he is a frequent contributor of photos and forestry-related articles to the Alabama Treasured Forest Magazine. He was the 2002 recipient of the Alabama Urban Forestry Association Award for Individual Achievement in Forestry, and the 2005 recipient of Auburn University's W. Kelly Mosley Environmental Award for "Achievements in Forestry, Wildlife and Related Resources." He is the author of Where the Wild Illicium Grows, a book on historic plants of the Central Gulf Coast.

String Lily, also called "Seven Sisters," *Crinum americanum*, are stunning in coastal marshes in the summer and fall.

Equally at home on shady river banks, in saltmarshes, and flower beds, Cardinalflower, *Lobelia cardinalis*, is thought by many to be America's most beautiful wildflower.

The Bog

Bogs are hot
and thorny
and ornery
places for sure.

by Fred Nation

Portfolio

South Alabama pitcher plant bogs are home to many rare and beautiful plants. Shown here are White-topped Pitcher Plants and White-fringed Orchids.

South Alabama Pitcher Plant Bogs

Pitcher plant bogs are without a doubt the thorniest, orneriest, cussedest places on the Gulf Coast. For starters, if it's not February, they are stifling hot. Bogs are open and nearly shadeless, surrounded by enveloping forests that block the flow of air. As you walk along, avoiding the wet spots, the catbriars, known locally as blaspheme-vines, close around you. As if possessed by some evil plant intelligence, the insidious briars attempt to saw your arms off or tear your shirt from your body. If you stumble into one of those wet spots, the odoriferous gray water that overtops your shoes and soaks

your clothes will not put you in mind of a rose garden. Then, there is the breathtaking beauty and the endless fascination of our magnificent gulf coast pitcher plant bogs, that makes their cussedness seem like a small price to pay for such splendor.

What makes a bog a bog and not something else? Bogs bring together an unusual combination of soil, water, and environmental conditions to create unique habitats. Many of the fascinating plants that make their homes in gulf coast pitcher plant bogs live nowhere else on earth!

Bog soils are sandy and porous, with very little organic material. Iron compounds cause the soil to be gray in color, which makes it

Above: White-topped Pitcher Plant, *Sarracenia leucophylla*. At right: Children love pitcher plants, possibly because "they are plants that eat animals!"

appear to be far richer than it is. In fact, coastal bog soils are highly acidic and quite poor in nutrients. This acidic, nutrient-poor soil is a key to the specialized plants that live in bogs. Since there is very little fertilizer in the soil, the plants have developed interesting and unusual ways to obtain necessary nutrients.

Carnivorous plants, such as pitcher plants and sundews, obtain nutrients by capturing and "eating" insects and other small creatures. Some bog plants, such as waxmyrtles, have the ability to "fix" atmospheric nitrogen in the soil by making use of special bacteria that grow on their roots. Lilies, grasses, and sedges are simply able to get-by with very low nutrient levels. They are well-adapted to the acidic, nutrient-poor soils that make bogs forbidding places for

plants that are not adapted to these harsh conditions.

Fire plays a crucial role in the health and survival of a bog. In fact, bogs are fire-dependent ecosystems. Without occasional fires to suppress the tree and shrub layers, the ground becomes shaded, and the sun-loving herbaceous plants decline and eventually die. Research indicates that before this area was settled, fires passed through coastal bogs two or three times in an average ten year period. These natural burns, caused by lightning, occurred mainly in the summer and fall. Fire suppression, increasing as our populations increase, is one of the biggest factors in the decline of our bogs. Since uncontrolled fires are now suppressed for safety reasons, programs of carefully managed controlled burns are crucial to safely

Purple Pitcher Plant, *Sarracenia purpurea*, known locally as "frog-britches!"

The golden flowers are Yellow-fringed Orchids, *Platanthera ciliaris*.

Opposite: Small insects become entangled in the pale green leaves of the carnivorous Gulf Coast Sundew, *Drosera tracyi*.
Below: Grasspink Orchid, *Colopogon pulchellos*, is a stunning native orchid in South Alabama Pitcher Plant bogs.

The beauty of the bog.

provide fire, as a natural and necessary element in the ecology of our pitcher plant bogs. Controlled burns also reduce the intensity of wildfires that would otherwise threaten our homes and businesses in fire-prone areas.

Bogs are wetlands, but they are not as wet as other wetland habitats, such as swamps and marshes. In fact, for a pitcher plant bog to remain healthy, it must become dry enough to burn occasionally. The water must be free from salt and nutrients, and the water table must come up to, or very near to the surface. If the water table is much higher, there will be standing water most of the time, and the habitat will then become a marsh or a swamp.

As you look out across coastal bogs, you will see some tall, white-colored tubular leaves. These are the "pitchers" of the glorious white-topped pitcher plant. Though they are still numerous in South Alabama, they are rare in the sense that they occur in a very restricted range, from near Appalachicola, Florida, along the coastal plain, to near the Louisiana state line. Because this plant is so pretty, with its white pitchers and large crimson flowers, it has been over-collected or even eradicated in some areas. Many bog visitors who have seen them in their natural habitats are convinced that white-topped pitcher plants are among the most fascinating and most beautiful plants on earth! Another of our five local pitcher plant species, and perhaps the most bizarre-looking, is the purple pitcher plant. One humorous local name for it is "frog britches!"

The tall, slender, pale-green leaves of a spectacular local carnivorous plant, the Gulf Coast sundew, has lovely pink flowers in the spring. Sundews produce a sticky substance on their leaves to capture and consume gnats and other small critters that land on them.

A dozen-or-so native orchids make their homes in South Alabama bogs. Some are quite rare, and a few are as spectacular in form and color as any of the world's flowers. The lovely, magenta-colored grasspink orchid blooms in late spring. Yellow-fringed orchid grows to three feet tall, with large, many-flowered masses of golden-colored flowers in midsummer.

In pre-European times thousands of pitcher plant acres were scattered throughout Mobile and Baldwin Counties. Most are gone now, beneath roads and shopping centers and subdivisions. The bogs that remain are special places, famous throughout the world for their vivid colors, dramatic shapes, and for the curious twist of nature that brings together a rare community of bizarre and wonderful plants that dine on animals.

Bogs are hot and thorny and ornery places for sure. But to those of us who love them, our pitcher plant bogs are the highest form of creation in the natural world. Other natural habitats are beautiful and interesting, but they were just practice!

Biography: Fred Nation

Fred Nation is a field botanist, freelance writer and photographer who lives in Daphne, Al. He teaches environmental subjects and "Plant Nomenclature" for the Baldwin and Mobile County Master Gardener intern classes, and for the Adult Learning Center in Fairhope. Fred conducts regular classes on habitats and ecosystems for the Volunteers at Weeks Bay Reserve. He has constructed interpreted nature trails for the City of Daphne, Blakeley State Park, Turtle Point Environmental Science Center (in Escambia County), and Camp Beckwith.

Fred has made many presentations for workshops and seminars for the USDA Forest Service, The Alabama Cooperative Extension System, and Weeks Bay Reserve. He is on the Board of Directors of Blakeley State Park and Mobile Botanical Gardens, and he is a member of the Baldwin County Environmental Advisory Board.

Fred has nominated or co-nominated 21 Alabama State Champion Trees in Baldwin County, and he is a frequent contributor of photos and forestry-related articles to the Alabama Treasured Forest Magazine. He was the 2002 recipient of the Alabama Urban Forestry Association Award for Individual Achievement in Forestry, and the 2005 recipient of Auburn University's W. Kelly Mosley Environmental Award for "Achievements in Forestry, Wildlife and Related Resources." He is the author of Where the Wild Illicium Grows, a book on historic plants of the Central Gulf Coast.

The Beach

Between the Land and the Water

by Maureen Nation

Portfolio

Seascape by Jeanne Ruff.

Landscaping the Transitional Zone

The transition zone, between the water's edge and the area where our landscapes begin, is a difficult place, requiring special attention and special plants. Scientists refer to this area, where the water meets the land, as the "littoral zone." By carefully selecting our plants, we can enhance and protect the natural shoreline, and at the same time provide a buffer from the harsh marine environments that can be detrimental to less tolerant plants in our landscapes. Careful littoral zone planting can slow run-off, reduce erosion, and filter pollutants as they enter our waterways. Plants in this zone also act as a

barrier from the water, by moderating the effects of wind, blowing sand, and salt spray on the rest of our landscape.

There are actually a couple of advantages to growing plants near large salty or brackish bodies of water. Extremes of heat and cold are moderated by water, which absorbs and releases heat much more slowly than the land. Because of this natural buffering, shorelines do not suffer the freezes of areas just a little farther inland. Salt spray also inhibits the growth of leaf-attacking fungi that often plague plants in our humid climate.

Growing plants in very poor soils or sand can present challenges to the home gardener, but once established, well-adapted

Sea Oats, *Uniola panicula*, play a crucial role in dune formation and stabilization on the Gulf Coast.

native plants, in particular, will thrive with only a little care. Contrary to conventional wisdom, to establish plants in sandy, fast draining soils, a hole deeper than the pot should be dug, and backfill should be amended with compost or peat moss. The plant should then be set a bit deeper in the hole than it was growing in the pot. One method used in beach restoration is to use a water-grabbing polymer mixed with water and a low nitrogen fertilizer placed in the bottom of the hole. The amendments will not persist, but will last long enough to help encourage stabilizing root growth.

Plants that have adapted to life in the transition zone are able to withstand intense sunlight, fierce winds laden with salt and sand, and intermittent droughts and floods. Some of the characteristics of these plants include: thick, grayish, or glasslike leaves; low-growing, sturdy stems and branches; and deep or fleshy roots, that can find and hold water and help anchor the plant to the shifting sands. Fortunately, many native trees, shrubs, and perennials, and some of our popular culinary herbs, are ideally suited to the littoral zone. Here is a short list of mostly native plants that will grow happily and look attractive, with little care, in the interesting but challenging area between the land and the water.

Beach Morning Glory, *Ipomoea imperati*, produces a daily crop of white flowers with golden centers. The roots help stabilize poor, granular soils.

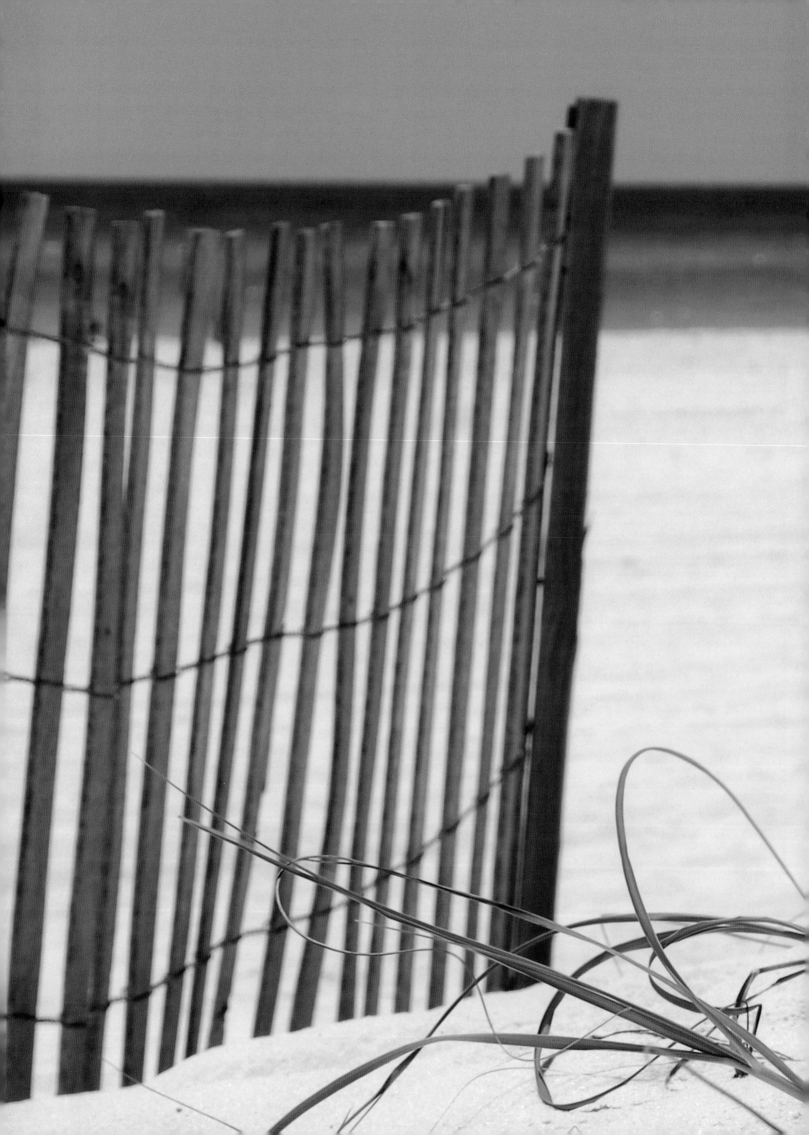

Tough Plants for Transition Zones

TREES

Live Oak	*Quercus virginiana*
Laurel Oak	*Quercus hemispherica*
Southern Magnolia	*Magnolia grandiflora*
Southern Redcedar	*Juniperus silicola*
Cabbage Palm	*Sabal palmetto*
Japanese Black Pine	*Pinus thunbergii*
Persimmon	*Diospyros virginiana*
Chaste Tree	*Vitex agnus-castus*

SHRUBS AND WOODY VINES

Yaupon	*Ilex vomitoria*
Southern Bayberry	*Myrica cerifera*
Gallberry	*Ilex glabra*
Wild Rosemary	*Conradina canescens*
Dahoon Holly	*Ilex cassine*
Groundsel	*Baccharis halmifolia*
Saw Palmetto	*Serenoa repens*
Beargrass	*Yucca filamentosa*
Oleander	*Nerium oleander*
Indian Hawthorn	*Rapheolepis indica*

Low-maintenance, drought-tolerant Pink Muhly Grass, *Muhlenbergia capillaris*, is one of our showiest native grasses.

Pittosporum	*Pittosporum tobira*	GRASSES	
Bottlebrush	*Callistemon rigidus*	Sea Oats	*Uniola paniculata*
Rosemary	*Rosmarinus officinalis*	Beach Panic Grass	*Panicum amarum*
Carolina Jasmine	*Gelsemium sempervirens*	Muhly Grass	*Muhlenbergia capillaris*
Shore Juniper	*Juniperus conferta*	Bushy Bluestem	*Andropogon glomeratus*

Above: A close-up of the blooms of the Moss Rose, *Portulaca grandiflora*. At right: Rosemary, *Rosmarinus officinalis*, is one of the great culinary herbs, and it can be easily grown on dry, sandy sites.

Biography: Maureen Nation

Maureen Nation is a life-long gardener and a Baldwin County Master Gardener for the past 16 years, and she was the 1998 recipient of the Wayne De la Rua award from the Baldwin County Master Gardener program. She has been recognized twice with certificates of appreciation for outstanding leadership to the Alabama Cooperative Extension System.

For the past 13 years Maureen has been on the staff of Weeks Bay National Estuarine Research Reserve, a state/federal agency whose mission is research, education and preservation of natural habitats in Baldwin County. Over the years Maureen has organized and conducted numerous workshops on the use of native plants in landscapes and habitat restoration projects. She has organized and managed a native plant sale at Weeks Bay Reserve for the past 15 years.

Since 1998 Maureen has been a member of the Board of Directors of the Village Point Foundation, a public service organization who secured the purchase of Bay Front Park and the Village Point Park Preserve, and continues to protect and develop these parks for public use.

Above: Our native Blanketflower, *Gaillardia pulchellos*, will add color and interest to beds in the transitional zone. Below: Saw palmetto, *Serenoa repens*, is a very tough customer in poor, sandy soils. Fruits are good forage for wildlife.

A typical transition-zone home landscape. Below: *Old Fence Line* by W.D. Thompson.

Rice by Louise Estes. Below: Seascape painting by Willoweise.

Moss Rose, *Portulaca grandiflora*, is a beautiful, drought-tolerant ground cover

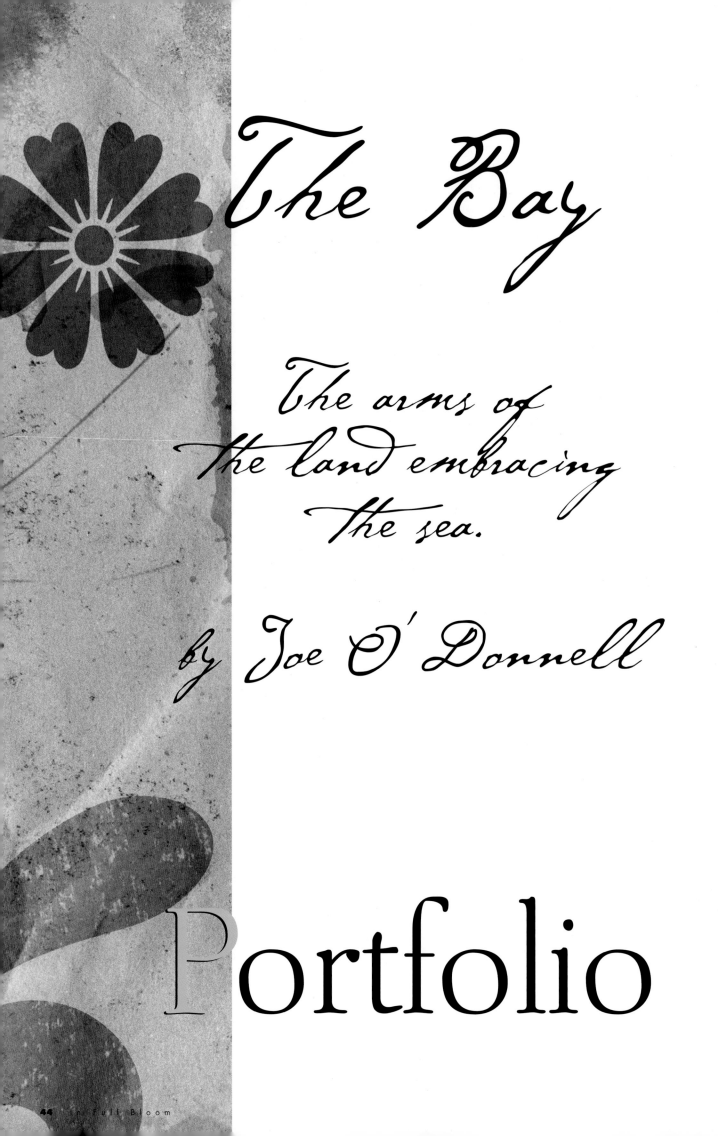

The Bay

The arms of the land embracing the sea.

by Joe O'Donnell

Portfolio

Down by the Bay. Photo by Stephen Savage.

Embracing the Sea

By Joe O'Donnell

The bay is quiet today, a breeze sweeping across and moving the water in a rippling arc toward the shore.

If you were to look at a bay from above—dropping down through the clouds in an airplane, or at the monitor of a computer accessing Google Earth for a satellite view—with an imaginative, almost childlike eye, you would see the outstretched arms of the land embracing the sea.

That is what makes a bay such a special place to live. It is friendly as a hug, touching as a quiet, emotional embrace.

Mobile Bay is just such a place—a wonder of special heartbeats, warm, embracing, welcoming.

The bay lies at the top of the Gulf of Mexico, formed by Fort Morgan Peninsula on the eastern side and Dauphin Island, a barrier island on the western side. The fourth largest estuary in the United States, Mobile Bay moves 62,000 cubic feet of water per second out into the Gulf.

Flowing from the Mobile River and Tensaw River, all that water empties into the northern reaches of the bay. These rivers are joined

Photograph by Brian Kasch

by smaller flows from the Dog River, Deer River, and Fowl River on the western side of the bay, and Fish River on the eastern side.

Four-hundred and thirteen square miles. Thirty-one miles long. Twenty-four miles wide at its largest girth. The shipping channel in the bay sinks to a depth in excess of 75 feet, but the average depth is about 10 feet.

The Spanish came here, cutting through the waves in their long ships, as early as 1500. Early Spanish maps called the area, the Bahía del Espíritu Santo (Bay of the Holy Spirit).

Hernando de Soto explored Mobile Bay in the mid-1500s, battling the Native Americans who had made their home on these shores for generations.

Although Spain's presence in the area had been on and off again for decades, the French created a deep-sea port at Dauphin Island

and founded French Louisiana's capital at Mobile in 1702.

From those roots, Mobile's role as a seaport continues even today. Now what is carried in those ships has certainly changed. In the 19th century, it was King Cotton, borne down through the South and out into open waters to a waiting world. Today the amount and variety of products that move through Mobile Bay to world markets is amazing.

When hostilities in Europe broke out in the mid-20th century, Mobile's shipbuilding industry and the city's population exploded.

The deep bay and the strategic harbor area have always been the main ingredients of Mobile's prosperity, but the waters of the bay have also been the elixir of beauty for this whole region. The bay is what makes Mobile different; like the leaf of a delicate flower or the fruit of beautiful vine it is the thing that makes it special.

For a sense of the special nature of the bay, just look at the Jubilee phenomenon of sea life gasping for air in the shallow waters of the bay—all ripe for the picking when people can gig hundreds of flounder or catch tubs of crabs in just a few hours.

Although jubilees have been reported in other areas, Mobile Bay is probably the only body of water in which this phenomenon occurs

fairly regularly, according to the Auburn University Marine Extension and Research Center. "It happens most often along the Bay's upper eastern shore from Great Point Clear to just north of Daphne. Jubilees also occasionally occur south of Point Clear to Mullet Point and on the western shore at Deer River and Dog River.

"Jubilees may affect the entire eastern shore from Daphne to Mullet Point, a distance of about 15 miles. Or, they may be limited to only a few hundred feet of beach. Jubilees are caused primarily by upwellings or upward movement of oxygenpoor bottom waters forcing bottom-type fish and crustaceans ashore. For a jubilee to take

place, a very specific set of conditions must exist. They occur only in the summer, usually in the early morning before sunrise. The previous day's weather conditions must include an overcast or cloudy day, a gentle wind from the east, and a calm or slick bay surface. Also, a rising tide is necessary; a change to a falling tide will stop the jubilee. It takes a combination of all these conditions to produce the phenomenon."

To create the phenomenon of the Mobile region (Mobile, Spanish Fort, Daphne, Fairhope, Point Clear, Montrose, Bon Secour) all it took was a bay.

Photograph by Brian Kasch

Photograph by Brian Kasch

Photograph by Brian Kasch

Photograph by Brian Kasch

FAIRHOPE

THE
*PURPLE MARTIN
RIVIERA*

226 CONDOS

ESTABLISHED 2001

Part Two

Bloom

Annuals

If Perennials Are the Backbone of Your Fower Garden, Then Annuals Are the "Fun and Fluff!"

By Lois Boykin

The best definition of an annual is plants that have to be replaced every year in your garden. Most annuals sprout from seeds, bloom, produce seeds and die within one season. Because we have a long growing season, some plants will self-sow, produce plants and bloom again in the same season. Zinnias, marigolds and cosmos are good examples of these annuals.

Most annuals need 4 to 6 hours of full sun. Some need full morning sun and shade in the hot afternoon. Annuals will not do well in an area that water stands in after a heavy rain, but most need regular watering. Prepare your beds and amend your soil before you plant. Turn your soil to a depth of 5 to 10 inches and mix bark humus, compost or leaf mold to improve drainage. If your soil has a lot of clay and packs badly, add sand and peat moss. A pH of 5.8 to 6.5 will make most annuals happy. Add lime if your soil is too acid. It is always a good idea to test your soil to see what it needs before planting anything!

Work fertilizer (10-10-10), according to directions, into the soil, rake the surface smooth and you are ready to plant. Annual plants are available or sow annual seed according to directions, depth, spacing and sowing time, on the packet. Always check the date on the packet to be sure you are starting out with fresh seeds. Fertilize plants again during the growing season. Foliage plants need 20-20-20 fertilizer. Keep spent flowers removed to encourage new growth and blooms. When plants start to look straggly, heavy pruning, feeding and watering will bring many annuals back to full attractive plants in just several weeks.

Some insects will attack annuals such as white flies, caterpillars, aphids, spider mites and slugs. Keep an eye out for pests and attack them before they have a chance to multiply. Keeping weeds under control will also help keep pests out.

Most annuals make great cut flowers. Cut them in the early morning. Some annuals self-sow better than others.

Annuals for Full Sun

African Daisy—upright, 4 to 12 inches high, narrow green leaves. Bloom colors: orange, yellow, violet, apricot, salmon

Calliopsis or *Coreopsis tinctoria*—upright, 1 to 3 feet high, small smooth green leaves, single and double bloom types, self-sow. Bloom colors: orange, yellow, bronze and maroon

Cosmos—upright, 2 to 8 feet high, bright green divided leaves, self-sow. Bloom colors: white, yellow, orange, pink, lavender, and multi-color

Cockscomb or Celosia—upright, 1 to 3 feet high, narrow green leaves, velvety, fan shaped flower clusters. Bloom colors: yellow, red, orange, purple

Coleus, sun coleus—upright, 1 to 2 feet high, roots easily, blue flower spikes, (keep pinched off). Grown for foliage in many colors: green, chartreuse, orange, red, salmon, purple, brown and multi colors

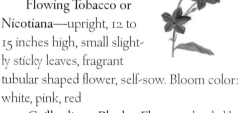

Flowing Tobacco or Nicotiana—upright, 12 to 15 inches high, small slightly sticky leaves, fragrant tubular shaped flower, self-sow. Bloom color: white, pink, red

Gaillardia or Blanket Flower—bush-like, 1 to 2 feet high, soft hairy green leaves, 2 inch wide flowers, self-sow. Bloom colors: red, yellow, gold

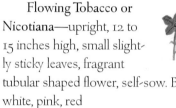

Gloriosa Daisy, Black-eye Susan or Rudbeckia hirta—upright, 3 to 7 feet high, hairy steams and pointed leaves. Bloom colors: yellow-orange with purplish-black centers

Joseph's Coat—branching, 4 to 6 inches high, foliage plant in shades of red and green

Melampodium—bush-type, 12 to 19 inches high, small green leaves, self-sow, and yellow daisy-like blooms

Moss Rose or Portulaca—low growing, 6-12 inches across, small, shiny and plump leaves, great for hanging basket, border and rock gardens, self-sow to a fault. Blooms: red, yellow, orange and white

Salvia- Texas sage—bushy, 2 to 3 feet high, dark green hairy leaves. Blooms: red and purple spikes

Spider Flower or Cleome—shrubby and branching, 4 to 6 feet high, divided green leaves, self-sow to a fault, long spike-like blooms that later form slender seed pods. Blooms: pink, purple and white

Sunflower—upright, 5 feet high, narrow green leaves large blooms of yellow petals and darker cushion of seeds in center

Verbena or Garden Verbena—branched, 6 to 12 inches high, spreading 1 to 3 feet wide, green to gray-green toothed leaves, flat clusters of flowers. Bloom colors: white, red, pink, purple, blue and combinations

Zinnia—upright, tall, 1 to 3 feet, compact to mini, 6 to 12 inches, narrow green leaves, self-sow, round blooms, flat to double. Color blooms: all the colors of the rainbow

Annuals for Sun or Part Shade

Ageratum—upright, heart shape green leaves, tall type-24 inches, dwarf type-4 to 6 inches, tassel-like clusters of flowers. Bloom colors: white, blue and pink

Begonia—shrubby, multi-colored foliage, waxy leaves, lacy clusters of flowers, bloom colors: red, white, and pink. There are many types of begonias. Some such as the Wax, Rex, Angle Wing, and the Iron Cross begonias are most often grown in containers as house plants. They can be considered tender perennials and must be protected from the cold.

Caladium—can be considered an annual or perennial. Tubers are planted when the ground becomes warm and are grown for their

foliage. The large heart shaped leaves grow in many colors; green, pink, red, bronze, pink, white, silver and combinations of colors. There are varieties that are bred for full sun and do very well here. A flower spike/seed will appear which will need to be pinched back to encourage the plant to put out new leaves. Some gardeners will dig the tubers and store for the winter. If tubers are left in the ground, some will rot from too

much water and cold but some can survive and grow for several years. However, the size of the leaf seems to diminish in time.

Coleus—see under Sun Annuals. There are coleuses that need part shade, and it is important when you are buying seeds or plants that you check to know which variety is which.

Impatiens—upright and bushy, small green pointed leaves, 6 to 24 inches high, 12 to 24 inches wide, flowers can be single or double, good container plant, self-sow, color blooms: purple, orange, red, pink, salmon, hot pink and white. Inpatients are a must for your shady area, are a "no fuss plant" and will be a mass of color from late spring until the first frost!

Torenia, Johnny Jump-up or Wishbone Flower—compact and bushy, narrow green leaves, tubular shaped flower with stamen arranged in a wishbone shape, self-sow. Color blooms: blue or white

Hardy Annuals

These annuals can be sown as seeds in the fall. The plants will come up, develop a root system, winter and reach maturity in the following spring or summer. If the temperatures fall below 25 degrees, mulch or cover for protection.

Cornflower or Bachelor's Button—upright, narrow gray-green leaves, 12 to 30 inches high, sun, shaggy full flower, self-sow. Color blooms: purple, pink and white

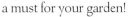

Foxglove or Digitalis—upright, hairy, gray-green leaves, 2 to 4 feet high, light shade, spires of tubular flowers, very dramatic long lasting blooms, sun, self-sow. Color blooms: white, pink, yellow and purple. Foxglove adds an English touch to the Southern garden!

Larkspur or Delphinium—upright, frilly dark green leaves, 12 to 36 inches high, full sun, long spikes densely set with double flowers, self-sow, sun. Color blooms: white, blue, pink, lilac, rose and salmon. This plant is a must for your garden!

Marigold—upright, robust free-branching, tall, 2 to 4 feet high, medium, 12 to 18 inches high, dwarf, 8 to 10 inches high, divided fern-like leaves with a strong aroma, full sun, self sow, round flowers are full to fully double, long lasting cut

flowers. Color blooms: yellow, orange, bronze to a combinations of mixed colors. Seems marigolds have been a long time favorite for our gardens, in fact, I would bet Scarlett O'Hara had a few in her garden.

Nasturtium—drooping bush, bright green "lollypop" leaves, 12 to 15 inches high, sun, fragrant eatable flowers (peppery taste) that can be used to garnish a dish or used in a salad. Color blooms: yellow, orange, reddish brown, maroon, and creamy white.

Poppy—upright, frilly gray-green leaves, 2 to 3 feet high, single or double flowers, some

with different colored centers, seed pods form as the flower falls off, self-sow, sun, very showy plants. Color blooms: red orange, yellow, salmon, pink, cream and white. Poppies will boom from March to May. You can use the pods for dried flower arrangements. You can bet you will have poppies for many years as they are notorious self-sowers!

Sweet Alyssum—low, branching trailing, green narrow lance-shaped leaves, 12 inches high, sun or light shade, tiny four- petaled clusters of flowers, fragrant, good border plant, self-

sow. Color blooms: white

Sweet Pea—vine, 5 plus feet or bush, 1 to 2 feet high,

small bright green leaves with runners, full sun to light shade, dragon head shaped flower with wings, very fragrant. Bloom colors: scarlet, purple, pink, cream and white. Sweet Peas are a southern favorite, lovely to cut and enjoy in your home!

Bedding Plants

These annuals can be planted as transplants in the early fall, late winter or early spring. The plants will develop their root systems and bloom in season. If they are planted in the fall, they may need to be covered or mulched if the temperature falls below 25 degrees.

Delphinium or Larkspur
(See in above section)

Dianthus or Sweet William—Upright, bushy, full morning sun and afternoon shade, 12 to 24 inches high, leaves are grass- like with tuffs of short spikes, clusters of single or double blooms, spicy fragrant. Bloom colors: pink, rose, red and multi-colored. A very old fashion favorite flower for your garden!

Ornamental Kale and Cabbage—Upright and bushy, 12 to18 inches high, prefers full sun and cool temperatures, grown for the foliage. Kale has ruffled edges and look like rosettes of green, pink, purple and white. Cabbage plants

begin leafy but will form loose heads. Leaves are dark blue green, edged with cream, white, purple or rose. Both are edible and are often used to garnish food. These plants add striking color and texture when mixed with other plants.

Foxglove or Digitalis
(See in above section)

Pansy or Viola—Short and bushy, 6 to 10 inches high, sun to part shade, dark green round leaves, face like flowers, fragrant. Bloom colors: many colors including bi-colors. Pansies are great for borders, containers and planted in mass. The perky faced pansies have been a long time favorite of southern gardens! Keep spent blooms pinched to keep your plants blooming.

Petunia—Trailing to bush, petunias prefer full sun to part shade and are great for baskets, containers or as bed-

ding plants. The leaves are medium green, broad and slightly sticky to the touch. The funnel shaped flowers that can be single, double or heavily ruffled, will give you pleasure from fall to summer if you keep the spent blooms pinched off. The bloom colors range from white to cream, pink to deep reds, light blue to deep purples and many bi-color combinations. Petunias have a delightful fragrant! The wave petunia has been bred to endure the summer heat and is wonderful for hanging baskets.

Calendula or Pot Marigold—Upright, 12 to 18 inches high, long, green, narrow, slightly sticky, fragrant leaves, full sun, round full flowers, bloom colors: orange, yellow and cream. Calendulas are excellent bedding plants as well as for use in containers. The common name, Pot Marigold, comes from an earlier use as a "pot herb"— seasoning for the vegetable pot.

Snapdragon—Upright and bushy, tall- 24 to 36 inches high, dwarf- 6 to 8 inches, small green leaves, full sun, five lobed flower shaped like "jaws" that will open when pinched, long narrow stems, fragrant. Color blooms: white, yellow, red, wine, pink, purple, and bi-color. Snapdragons, a long time favorite annual, make excellent cut flowers. Dwarf varieties make a wonderful border and any variety planted in mass adds sparkle to you flower bed! Children are drawn to this "snapping flower"!

Stock—Upright, 12 to 18 inches high, narrow grey-green leaves, full sun to light shade, very fragrant, flowers grow in spike-like clusters on long stems. Bloom colors: cream, yellow, white, red, pink, purple and lavender. Stock is an excellent cut flower and has a delightful fragrant. Stock blooms will make a bold statement in any garden!

Many Hardy Annuals will die when our hot summer sun over takes them. As a rule, most of these annuals have a long blooming season and are a wonderful addition to you fall, winter and spring garden.

Annual that attract Hummingbirds and Butterflies

Ageratum, Calliopsis Cosmos, Gaillardia, Nasturtium, Nicotiana, Salvia, Verbena, Zinnia.

Perennials

Perennials Are the Backbone of Our Southern Flower Gardens and Are Often Referred to as Herbaceous Perennial Flowers

By Lois Boykin

Most Perennials will grow and flower for several years so this is why you must plan and prepare your beds before you plant them. Many perennials have a shorter blooming season than annuals as they must store up energy to return and bloom again. Some perennials have colorful foliage and seed pods to add interest after the blooms are spent. Perennials will go dormant in the winter but will emerge again from the crown or roots in the spring. Because of our hot summers, some plants that are considered perennials in other areas, will act as annuals here because they cannot take the hot sun. If you mix perennials with your annuals you can have blooms almost year round in your garden. Remember to add some potted perennials to your deck, patio or yard for added color and accents.

Here are some facts and ideas to consider before you plant perennials:

↣ Shade or sun: If shade or partial shade is required, and you are planting under a tree, remember that as tree roots grow they may compete with the perennials for moisture.

↣ Slope and drainage: Most perennials prefer well drained soil. Some plants will tolerate short periods of heavy moisture but will die if allowed to have "wet feet" for an extended time. Most perennials like regular watering.

↣ Soil: Most perennials prefer a soil pH of 5.5 to 6.5. Lime can be added to raise the pH. Incorporate 3 to 4 inches of organic matter, such as compost or mulch, into the soil before planting.

↣ Food: Fertilize perennials with 5-10-10. Work fertilizer into the soil before plants are put into the grown. Fertilize again when plants began to bloom.

↣ Mulch: Mulch plants to help the soil retain moisture and control weeds.

↣ Appearance: Consider color, foliage, textures, height and width and growth habit of plant. Consider the season of bloom. Some perennials have showy blooms while others have more interesting foliage. Short growing plants are great for borders as well in rock gardens. Tall plants will make great back ground and mix well with annuals and shrubs.

↣ Seeds or plants: Perennial plants that are planted in the early fall, will establish their roots, die back in the winter, return in the spring and bloom in season. Plants that are planted in the spring will bloom in season. Perennial seeds planted in the ground in the spring will come up and grow but usually will not bloom until the following year. You may start your seeds in a green house in the summer to be put out in the early fall. Plants will die back and reappear in the spring. Allow room for the plants to develop and mature. To make new plants, perennial can be divided at the roots in the fall or early spring.

↣ Share extra perennials with a friend!

Listed are some perennials that do well in our area but by no means does this list include all that will thrive and grow here. Check your garden centers for new plants that might be on the market and ask your fellow gardener for suggestions. One of the best opportunities to gather new and old plants, get advice and to commune with fellow gardeners is the plant sale sponsored by the Master Gardeners of Mobile and Baldwin County. There are sales in the spring and fall.

Calla Lily *Zantedeschia spp.*

The common Calla lily is basically an evergreen that usually goes dormant in the winter. It grows best in well drained soil, partial shade and needs regular water during growth and blooming time. The leaves are a rich glossy green, arrow shaped and grow from a bulb. Plants will grow to about three feet and have cup like blooms in the summer. Blooms are in shades of pink, yellow and white. Calla lilies do well in containers.

Chrysanthemum (Mum) *Chrysanthemum morifolium*

There are over 160 species of Chrysanthemums, mostly native to Japan, China and Europe. This plant has a fragrance all its own and it is hard to describe! The blooms come in many shapes; pompom, single or daisy, semi-double, spider, spoon, quill, and brush to name a few. There is almost no limit to the bloom colors—the sky is the limit! Most of us associate chrysanthemums with the fall of the year and maybe football season. Remember the corsages made from chrysanthemums in your school colors? When you see chrysanthemums in the garden centers, you know fall is just around the corner.

Chrysanthemums are easy to grow! Set young plants out in the spring in well drained, enriched soil in full sun or in some shade from the hot afternoon sun. Plants in full sun will of course need extra water. Too much water will cause leaves to yellow, turn black and drop. Too little water will causes woody stems, leaves to dry and drop. Established plants that bloomed in the fall will need to be cut back and can be divided at this time and moved to a new location. Fertilize two to three times in the growing season, the last application with low nitrogen fertilizer not less than two weeks before the buds break.

Now, some gardeners allow the established plants to grow, bud and bloom in the early summer cutting them back again to re-grow and bloom in the late fall. This practice does not allow the plants to produce large flowers but it does allow for blooms twice a year.

When you plant already established and ready to bloom plants in the fall, remember to soak the plant roots well before planting. You can turn a tired looking flower bed into a mass of color in no time. Now sit back, enjoy and know that fall and cool weather is on the way!

Canna lily *Canna x generalis*

Most of the old Southern gardens had several clumps of Cannas. This tuberous-rooted perennial adds a tropical look to any flower bed. Canna Lilies have large lance shaped leaves, much like a banana plant, and range in color from green, orange-red, purple-tinted to variegate. The blooms are large spikes clustered in heads at the top of a tall stem in bold colors of red, orange, yellow, coral, ivory and bi-colored. Growing best in moist humus-rich soil and full sun, these plants can reach from four to seven feet tall. In the early spring, cut back the dead leaves and mulch to hold the moisture. The blooms usually appear in the early summer and will bloom for weeks. Cannas may be raised from seed but it is faster to divide the roots in the early spring. Cannas multiply easily.

Tickseed *Coreopsis grandiflora*

Coreopsis can be both an annual and perennial depending on the variety. Tickseed, a perennial, is an easy plant to grow and will give you pleasure year after year. The golden yellow blooms appear in the early summer and will continue to bloom into fall. Plant in full sun in well drained soil. Plants will reach about 18 inches high and about 20 inches wide. Coreopsis plants can be planted or divided in the spring or fall. Leave plants until frost collapses them, and then cut back.

There are many varieties of coreopsis, such as lanceleaf and threadleaf that produce a wide variety of colors. Keep your eyes open and try several varieties, you will enjoy them.

Dusty Miller *Senecio cineraria*

Dusty Miller provides delightful silver foliage with lacy leaves. It complements and softens when planted with other annuals and perennials. It prefers full sun, well drained moderate fertile soil and regular water. It will grow about 12 to 24 inches high and wide. In the second year of growth, clustered heads of yellow will appear and last for weeks. If the plant gets leggy, cut the foliage back. This plant can be found in most garden centers in the fall, spring and summer. Some gardeners will treat Duster Miller as an annual, pulling it up at the end of summer so they never get to see the wonderful yellow blooms.

Gaura *Gaura lindheimeri (white)*

Gaura is native To Texas and Louisiana. It is an airy plant growing 2 to 4 feet high. It is an eye catching plant that produces spike-like flowers. Pink and white forms of Gaura are available. It blooms from late spring to late summer. Plants prefer full sun, fertile well-drained soil but tolerate light afternoon shade and humidity. Gaura can be planted in the spring or fall leaving growth until frost wilts it back, then cut back.

Gazania Daisy (Treasure Flower) *Gazania hybrida*

The Gazania Daisy is native to South Africa. They are near-evergreen, low growing plants with two basic types: clumping or trailing. They like sun and will grow in most soil that is well drained. Divide or plant in the spring and feed once with a slow-acting fertilizer. The leaves are narrow and green, most often with a silver or lighter color underneath. Plants are available in single colors of, white, yellow, orange, rosy pink and a reddish purple. Other plants are a mixture of colors with bands, stripes and eyes of a different color. These plants offer a combination for everyone giving dazzling color to your garden from spring to fall!

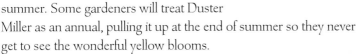

Gerbera Daisy *Gerbera jamesonii*

One word can describe this daisy— elegant! This flower is used often in arrangements and the blooms will actually last weeks. The plant itself is also showy. The lobed rich colored leaves can reach as

long as 10 inches, springing from a root crown that spreads slowly to form a large clump. The flower looks as though it rises from the ground. The many, many colors are vivid to pastels and really make a statement in your garden. Gerberas bloom most of the year dying back in cold winters. Cut off dead leaves and the warming spring sun will bring them right back up.

Gerberas have to have well drained soil, in sun or partial shade. Do not plant below the crown of the plant as this will keep it from blooming and can even kill the plant. Plant in the spring or fall, water regular, remove old leaves and spent blooms and fertilize every month. Give new plants a little extra water in the hot weather until the roots become established.

Don't be surprised if the plant wilts when it gets too dry until the plant is established. This daisy will be one of your favorite flowers in the garden. And, don't forget to enjoy the blooms in your home!

Geranium *Pelargonium*

Geraniums are a Southern favorite not only as bedding plants but as container plants. Because the geranium is a "true Southern Lady" she likes a little shade from the hot summer sun! For this reason, most of us like to grow our geraniums in pots or window boxes. There are many species, some that are bush like and some trailing with ivy shaped leaves. The blooms can be single or clusters but each will have five overlapping petals, two point in one direction and the other three point in the opposite direction.

Geraniums like well drained soil and regular water. You might want to plant them in the spring, as they do their best in the cooler weather and where they are protected from the heat. Bloom colors range from white to red to shades of pink and coral and violet to purple. There are even some blooms that are variegated in color. Other plants have leaves that are scented to smell like lemons, peppermint and roses.

Gladiolus (Glads) *Gladiolus byzantinus*

Describing a Glad is easy; a tall straight stem, sword-shaped leaves up both sides with lovely, long ruffled spikes of color at the top. This is a superb cut flower for the home. Glads come in many colors and are even variegated.

Plant the corms (bulb-like) in the spring, planting several at a time for several weeks. This way you will have blooms for months. Plant corms in the sun in well-drained sandy soil about 4 times deeper than their height and plant them somewhat more shallowly in heavy soil. Space corms in the soil about 6 inches apart. Water plants regularly while they are growing and blooming. Leave the stalk attached to the corms until it dies as this is where the corm receives its food for next year's blooms. Corms bloom about 65 days after planting.

Here on the coast, wild glades grow in many yards and along the highway. They have only orange blooms. The story goes that they came from Europe many, many years ago and survived all these years spreading all over this area in large numbers. They are very hardy and multiply vigorously.

Pentas (Star Clusters) *Rubiaceae*

Butterflies and hummingbirds are attracted to the flowers on the Pentas plant. Grown in sun or partial shade, this plant likes moist, fertile and well drained soil. This bush type plant will reach 2 to 3 feet tall. The leaves are long and somewhat hairy. The blooms are showy 4 inch wide clusters of small star-shaped flowers in red, lilac, pink and white. Feed monthly and remove the dead flowers to encourage a long blooming season. The flowers are suitable for cutting.

Salvia *Salvia xsuperba*

The many species of salvia can be annuals, biennials, perennials or shrubs coming from many countries. Most varieties do well in our area and can be found in the local garden centers. Perennial Salvia is also known as hybrid sage. They like well drained, moderately fertile soil and full sun. The leaves are green to silver depending on the variety and the long spike blooms are white, violet or purple. They grow upright getting 24 to 36 inches high and 18 to 24 inches wide and like moderate water. Divide roots every three years in the spring to keep the plants healthy. Salvia is a showy plant, requiring very little care, so try several varieties.

Scabious

(Pincushion Flower) *Scabious columbaria*

This plant is called a pincushion because that's exactly what the blooms look like. Stamens stick up from the round flower head, giving the appearance of a pin cushion. The blooms can vary from blue to bluish lavender or white

and are on wiry steams. Blooming will begin in the mid-summer and will bloom until fall if you keep the old blooms cut. The blooms make excellent cut flowers. The plants are heat tolerant and do best in well drained soil with moderate water. Prune back in the fall once frost has killed back the foliage. Plants may be divided at the roots and plants will re-seed themselves.

Succulent

There are many species of succulents. They come from many parts of the world and are very hardy plants. They come in as many shapes as you can image. Some are tiny, fat, tall, complex, trailing to just plain funny looking. The leaves are fleshy and vary in color and most of the time evergreen. Flowers are usually small, star like, blooming in clusters at the top of long stems. Some flowers are brightly colored and blooms will last a long time. Succulents root so easily that you can lay a leaf in soil and it will sprout roots. Do not over water for as a rule they like to stay a little dry.

These plants will do well in the sun to part shade and are well suited to rock gardens and container gardens. Plants need to be in well drained soil or in pot or containers that drain well.

Many gardeners collect succulents and trade with others. Because some are so unique and hardy, they make wonderful plants for children.

One of the largest succulents is the Century Plant (Agave Americana) reaching a height of 6 plus feet. It takes many years (about 10) for the Century plant to bloom. The blooms are clusters of yellow funnel-shaped flowers on long stems. The Century Plant is not a real friendly plant as it does have leaves with sharp thorn-like edges along the sides. Given its own space, this plant can be a real attraction in a yard.

One variety of Succulent is Sedum and there are many varieties of these. One of the better know in our area is Autumn Joy. Planted in full sun, this sedum will reach 24 inches high and 24inches wide. You can plant them in the spring or fall in moderate fertile, well drained soil. Plants planted in the spring will flower in mid-summer. Blooms will appear pink, and then a rose red to finally in the fall a deep burgundy. The flowers attract the bees and butterflies. Stems can be rooted or the roots can be divided to make new plants. Prune back dead foliage in the spring before the plant begins to put out. Autumn Joy makes a great container plant for your deck and yard.

Agapanthus (African lily, Lily-of-the-Nile) *Agapanthus cultrivars*

The Agapanthus plant has become very popular in the last ten years here on the coast. It is a member of the onion family but does not produce a true bulb. These plants have strap shaped leaves, from which rise a bare stem ending with a cluster of bell-shaped flowers that could remind you of a burst of fireworks. The blooms range from white to blue to almost a violet color. They bloom in the early summer.

These plants will grow and bloom in full sun as well as light shade. They grow best in loamy, well drained soil and can tolerate prolonged dry spells. Agapanthus is deciduous but in a mild winter, plants may not die back. They make a lovely border for a bed due to their narrow upright shape. Plants like to be root bound but can be divided every five to six years to make new plants or shared with a friend.

These striking blooms will last several weeks and make a show in your garden. Remove the spent flower heads to encourage further blooming. The dwarf forms of agapanthus do well in rock gardens or planted in containers. This plant will give you joy for many years with little effort.

Shasta daisy *Leucanthemun x superbum*

The Shasta daisy has always been a long time favorite of the Southern gardens. The flower, white petals with a yellow center is like sunshine or a happy face growing in your garden. Most young girls have plucked each petal citing "he loves me, he loves me not" to help decide if that boy in her life is for real or not!

Shasta daisy prefers full sun to part shade from the afternoon sun and moderately fertile, well drained soil. Water deeply when the soil is dry. These excellent cutting flowers bloom from early summer to fall. Deadhead spent flowers to encourage re-blooming. Clumped, upright plants grow 36 inches high to 24 inches wide and need to be divided every 2 to 3 years in the spring or fall. Plants are well suited for borders or containers.

Rudbeckia (Coneflower) *Asteraceae (Compositae)*

The garden rudbeckia is a descendant of wild plants native to North America sometimes known as a Black-eyed –Susan. The plants are easy to grow and will thrive most anywhere except in soggy soil. They like sun but will do well in partial shade with moderate water. There are several varieties, some getting 24 inches to 36 inches high with very large flowers of yellow to orange. The blooms will last for weeks and make great cut flowers. Divide the plants every 2 to 3 years or when they become overcrowded. Rudbeckia will wake any garden up!

Phlox (Thrift) *Polemoniaceae*

Phlox is a showy perennial that varies by species. Foliage ranges in colors from green to variegated and in height from tall to dwarf. Some varieties work well in rock gardens such as the everlasting creeping phlox or thrift. In many of the old, old, old gardens the waves of pink thrift were one of the first perennials to announce Spring is on the way!

Blooms are clusters of flowers that run from coral to pink, purple to lavender, and white. Phlox grow well in average garden soil, in sun to partial shade, needing average water. Plants grow from 2 to 4 feet high and 1 to 3 feet wide. Creeping phlox can cover an area in no time. The upright plants will bloom from summer to fall. Plants can be divided in the spring or fall when they become too thick. Butterflies and hummingbirds are attracted to this plant. You will want to try many varieties of Phlox in your garden!

Verbena *Vebenaceae*

Verbena makes a great plant for a hanging basket, ground cover, and the taller sorts are great in borders. Here again there are many species of verbena. One of the most popular is Homestead. It has long popsicle shaped clusters of flowers that stay showy for a long time. Verbena likes full sun, moderate fertile, well drained soil with regular water. Most thrive in heat and drought conditions Plants may be upright or running depending on variety. The low growing plant will send out runners making this variety best for hanging baskets and containers. Blooms range in colors of red, pink, white and purple and will flower from spring to fall. Some blooms can be multi-colored depending on variety. Dead head spent flowers to encourage blooming.

Vinca (Periwinkle) *Apocynacaeae*

Vinca: a tried and true, never failing garden friend that prefers partial shade to full shade. Full sun will be tolerated if soil is kept moist. Plants are low growing with shinny dark green leaves. Blue to lavender, five-pedaled pinwheel shaped flowers appear in the leaf joints in the spring and will bloom all summer and into the fall. As the plants are low growing, plants will layer root where the nodes touch the ground. This is a plant to enjoy!

Yarrow *Achillea spp.*

Here today, Yarrow tomorrow! Yarrow is one of the most care-free growing perennial, blooming from summer to fall. However, yarrow will spread! So plant in an area that you will want covered in a short time. Plants can be pulled up and transplanted most any time from spring to fall. Plants have long roots that tend to run.

There are several varieties of yarrow that produce blooms of yellow, white, rose to red. The fern-like and silky leaves can be gray to green. The blooms appear on long steams and are flattish clusters that can measure 1 to 10 inches wide. Blooms will last well and even make great cut flowers. Some yarrow can be dried for arrangements.

Plants like full sun, average well drained soil, and medium to dry moisture. Yarrow is an upright plant that will average 36 inches high and 18 inches wide. Yarrow makes a great plant for your butterfly garden.

Above: Resurrection Fern, *Pleopeltis polypodioides*, is an epiphyte that grows harmlessly on the bark of large trees. Leaves wither during drought, become plump and green after rain.

Ferns

ADIANTUM CAPILLUS-VENERIS
SOUTHERN MAIDEN

CHROMIUM FALCATE
JAPANESE HOLLY

DRYOPTERIS ERYTHROSORA
SOUTHERN SHIELD

Let's Talk Ferns

By Joan M. Thorington

Ferns vary from size, sun and shade requirements and come in a variety of shades of green, bronze and even variegated. The right fern strategically placed can enhance anyone's filtered sun garden. Diverse and equally reliable ferns can look healthy from early spring to late fall in our coastal Alabama yards. Let's not forget, ferns have adapted and survived on this planet for a long time while other species have disappeared.

Some ferns are called terrestrial which means they are found in woodlands, fields, marshes and mountains. Others have attached themselves to trees becoming what is called epiphytic. The other group of ferns found in lakes and ponds are naturally called aquatic ferns.

The three I have the most success with in my filtered environment are the southern Maiden (*Adiantum capillus-veneris*), the southern Shield (*Dryopteris erythrosora*) and the Japanese Holly

(*Chromium falcate*). The southern Maiden fern works well as an indoor plant. This fern is delicate but hearty and if you keep it moist and away from cold or heat draft it will soften the room wherever you place it. A bright indirect light source, a moist, loose potting medium and a saucer underneath filled with water will encourage your maiden to do well as an indoor plant. Give the maiden fern the same care you do your African violets and it will be pleased.

The Japanese Holly ferns are a great performer in a yard with filtered sunlight and are easily recognized by its dark green, shiny and leathery looking fronds. There are visible brown spores on the underneath side of the leaves and if this fern has found its ideal location in your landscape it can grow to three feet in both directions. The Japanese Holly and the Southern "Autumn" ferns prefer to be planted outside whereas the Maiden can be an indoor or outdoor fern. If you are mixing your own soil for your indoor ferns you can't go wrong with American Violet soil. Apply water soluble fertilizer once a month from spring to fall and when you water them they like the water temperature to be warm and not cold.

My choice for an outstanding performer outdoors is the Southern Shield or "autumn" fern. This is a tufted plant with arching fronds that can reach over three feet in length .With its mixture of

Above: Bracken Fern, *Pteridium aquilinum*, one of the world's most widespread plants, is at home in the South Alabama pineywoods.

green and coppery foliage it can keep this healthy appearance all year with some minor protection. Some landscapers will occasionally over plant this fern due to their carefree (minor snipping of old fronds) nature and performance. When planted this way, it detracts from the true beauty of this plant. Not many ferns grow well when crowded, and if too many are planted too closely together they will get tall, sparse and lanky. With enough space and planted alone or in groups of three (allowing at least four feet in between) these ferns will enhance the appearance of any filtered sun garden. Ferns are a

great addition to rock gardens providing us with different colors and textures. So don't be fearful of ferns, let them become your next best friend in your garden!

Biography: Joan M. Thorington

To write about oneself can be somewhat difficult, "tooting your own horn" so to speak so let's start 58 years ago. I was born Sharron Lee Leyh in Germany and at 3 1/2 I was adopted by Air Force parents who were stationed in London. At the age of 5 we moved back to the states, A name change, Joan McFall Thorington (Joni to my friends), a natu-

Above: Ferns make a beautiful accompaniment to any garden scene. Opposite: Native ferns create a cool, lush atmosphere in shady natural areas.

ralization process to become a citizen and my first participation in a flower show followed, I still have that first place ribbon in my jewelry box. And with great delight at the age of 9 the Camellia Society of South Carolina named a pink camellia after me.

Several years and many competitive swim meets later at the age of 13 I fell, severely breaking my ankle. The swim meets and aspirations of the Olympics went out the window so I went back to my first love, plants! Assisting my grandmother with her prize winning Dahlias and my mother's constant search for as many plants she could find in shades of lavender. I was also given recognition on several occasions for "yard of the month" wherever we were stationed.

I graduated from a boarding school in North Carolina, attended classes at Aum and Huntingdon College in Montgomery, Alabama. I graduated with a degree in Fine Arts from Faulkner and finished my education at the University of South Alabama in Mobile. Recognized as a fine arts photographer I sold my limited edition black & white photographs across the southeast with permament collections of my works in Louisianna, Mississippi, Alabama, Florida and Georgia.

Fast forwarding through my debutante and junior league years I have a son who is 35 and lives with his wife in Montgomery, Alabama and I have lived in Fairhope, Alabama for 30 years. My attraction and awe of "mother earth's flora" was implanted as a young child by my Mother and Grandmother and continues to this day. I am employed by Jim Preast at Preast's Petals & Pottery on Gayfer Ext. in Fairhope, Alabama. I adore my job and truly enjoy sharing my knowledge and affection of plants with friends and frequent customers.

Iris

Nita's Iris by Carolyn Newcomer.

Growing Iris on the Gulf Coast

By Judy Lucci

There are countless species and hybrids of Iris in practically every color imaginable. Many are suitable for Gulf Coast gardens. They range from delicate ground covers to elegant Bearded or Japanese varieties that are well over three feet tall.

Iris species are comprised of two varieties: Those growing from rhizomes and from bulbs. Both species can be successfully grown on the Gulf Coast. The authoritative source for detailed information about growing Iris in the South is the Clemson University Home and Garden Information Center (http:hgic.clemson.edu)

The most spectacular plants produced from Rhizomes are the Japanese and bearded varieties. The bearded varieties are typified by sword shaped leaves and strong stocks usually bearing more than one flower. Ruffled 6-8 inch flowers have showy upright petals as well as drooping petals, frequently of contrasting or complimentary color. The drooping petals are topped by hairy appendages thus, "bearded iris." Japanese iris have a somewhat different beardless flower form. Wide varieties of reblooming bearded iris have recently become available and are suitable for Southern gardens; three popular varieties are Dante's Inferno, Champagne Elegance and Pink Attraction.

Bearded irises prefer 8 hours full sun during the growing season. However in the Deep South, partial shade in the afternoon is

preferable because of the heat. New bearded iris should be planted in the early fall so that the plants will have an opportunity to establish themselves before the end of the growing season. Very specific procedures should be followed in the planting of iris rhizomes. The rhizome itself should be placed barely beneath the surface but the roots should be placed deeply in adjacent well conditioned soil. Care

should be taken not to over fertilize. Over fertilized plants do not bloom.

Other Iris varieties successfully grown on the Gulf Coast include the following:

⚐ Common Flag: The yellow or purple variety is the descendent of the "Fleur de Lis." Preferring acid neutral soil, this variety is common in marshes and along creek beds and other afternoon shade site. It is adaptable to growing in shallow water and is often a feature in water gardens.

⚐ Dutch Iris: The most popular Dutch hybrid adapted to the South is "Wedgewood." It is an early bloomer with large lavender/blue petals and yellow markings

⚐ Louisiana Iris: Prominent on the Gulf Coast because of its adaptability to hot weather and pest resistance. The most common popular hybrid, (*Brevicoulis i.floriosa*).

⚐ Siberian Iris: Emerging from rhizomes, these elegant beard-less flowers are hybrids derived from subirica and sanguiea varieties. Colors include white, shades of blue, and lavender, purple, wine, pink and light yellow. Partial shade and acid neutral soil are preferred. These irises have a unique grass like foliage. Neomanica gracillus is a widely popular variety.

⚐ Walking Iris: This is a tropical iris variety that may be grown on the Gulf Coast if heavily mulched and protected from frost. The name is derived from the variety's habit of producing roots where ever stocks touch the soil. Full sun or partial shade is preferred. Plants develop in clumps, leaves taking on a fan like shape. Stems are two feet long topped by white flowers with blue markings.

Irises are low maintenance, relatively pest free, long lived perennials. Share or trade varieties with friends.

Yellow Iris by Kay Godshalk

Hemerocallis "Dutch Yellow Truffle" (Kirchoff, D 2003)

Daylilies

Hemerocallis "Christmas Beau" (Petit, T 2004)

A Perennial Favorite

By John Falck

Daylilies have been garden favorites for many years because of their beauty and durability. Even so, many gardeners don't realize the wide variety beyond the usual oranges and yellows of a grandparent's yard. Today, daylilies come in sizes from miniatures measuring about an inch to spiders about 10 inches in diameter. They often rebloom one or more times per season. They add beauty, attract butterflies and hummingbirds, and even provide erosion control.

Forms include round, star shaped, spider, double and many combined forms. Colors range from near white to near black. Patterns include not only eyes and edges, but also intricate appliquéd patterns of multicolors. Bloom heights begin at about 12 inches to over 35 inches. These many possibilities make daylilies ideal choices for all parts of a garden.

Although daylilies perform best in full sun with plenty of water, they will grow in shade and survive drought conditions. Best planted in the fall or early spring to ensure good bloom for the next season, they prefer sandy loam soil with plenty of humus material. Space plants 18-24 inches apart to allow room for growth into nice clumps. The planting hole can be enhanced with a time release fertilizer, organic fertilizer, alfalfa pellets, and repeat the fertilizing with time release, milorganite, and Epsom salts in late February or early March to give the plants a boost for spring.

If the plant is root, prepare a hole wide enough to spread the roots. For a potted plant, lift out of the pot and spread the roots (you may have to use a knife to cut through roots to loosen them up). Place a small mound in the center of the hole. Place the center "crown" of the plant on the mound and arrange the roots in a circle around the center. Fill the hole up to the top of the white and beginning of the green on the main plant. Tamp the soil in to get air pockets out of the soil. Top dress with fertilizer and Epsom salts. Water thoroughly after planting. Continue the watering daily until the plant shows new

Above left: *Hemerocallis* "Symphony of Praise" (Bell, T 2003). Above right: *Hemerocallis* "John Peat" (Peit, T 2001). Below: *Hemerocallis* "Crystelle's Love" (Grace-Smith 2004).

growth from the center of the fan.

Maintenance includes watering at least inches a week, preferably by watering at least every two to three days. You can use a sprayed balanced fertilizer mixed with the water every one to two weeks during bloom to enhance bloom. Plants like mulch to keep soil cool and damp during the hot months. Deadheading helps the looks of the plant but does not encourage more blooms as buds are set on the scape (stem) when it is formed. Spent scapes may be cut near the base when they complete blooming for appearance. Do not pull out as they come from the growing center of the plant.

Daylilies are a colorful addition to any garden. They are effectively grown as specimen plants, in borders, as background plants, or in mixes with other plants. Their wide range of color makes them effective in all color combinations. Also, they can be used in contain-ers alone or with other plants. Thus, the variety and the versatility of daylilies make them a favorite garden perennial.

To learn more about daylilies you can go to the American Hemerocallis website: www.daylilies.org

Biography: John Falck

Born in Mobile and raised in Fairhope, John Falck spent his working career as a social studies teacher, assistant principal, and principal at Fairhope and Robertsdale High Schools. His interest in daylilies began with helping his father who was an enthusiastic gardener. When his father's health failed, he began taking over his dad's small daylily nursery. The nursery has grown to a large operation selling locally and on the internet. He is also Regional Vice President of Region 14 (Alabama and Mississippi) of the American Hemerocallis Society. Today he and his wife Nancy are working to develop and introduce their own "fancy" large and double daylilies.

Below: *Hemerocallis* "Tuscawilla Snowdrift" (Hansen R 2000).

Above left: *Hemerocallis* "Pure Indulgence" (Carr, R 2000). Below left: *Hemerocallis* "Morning Colors" (Stamile, P 2005). At right: *Hemerocallis* "Morning Colors" (Salter, EH 2005).

Elephant Ears

When I Mention Elephant Ears, Most People Want to Turn and Run.

By Virginia Boehme, Fairie Tale Orchids

We tend to think of Elephant Ears as "out of control" or "runners." This fear can rob gardeners of golden opportunities to impliment unusual character to their landscape. Once the gardener understands the different varieites that are available, the possibilities are endless.

All are hardy to 45 degrees before they begin to show signs of wanting to go dormant. You can avoid the dormancy period by bring-ing them into a warmer climate. Either is fine. They begin coming out of dormancy around 45 degrees, but the foliage will still be tender to sudden drops in temperatures.

Elephant Ears are great for container gardening. Just be aware that your container size dictates the size that your Elephant Ear will be able to grow. The recommended container size is 7 gallons or larger. This container can be left in the garden through winter.

The beginning leaves can look entirely different than the mature leaves. It takes until about the 5th leaf before you begin seeing the true character of the plant. Changes that can be expected: Size of leaf, edes can become ruffled, and sometimes color changes.

There are 3 types of Elephant Ears. Alocasia, Colocasia and Xanthosoma. Each variety has different growing habits.

Alocasia

Alocasia is the largest of the Elephant Ear family. This variety does not run, ever. Alocasias clump. You have to dig up the parent plant to separate the babies. Then you replant the parent plant.

This variety is the last to come out of dormancy. They are mostly used as container plants, one of the most common, The African Mask. It is mainly used as a houseplant. Gardeners rarely use Alocasias planted in the garden. However, there are several that are very happy in the ground. Example: Green Shield, Cuculllata, Portodora.

Alocasias offer upright leaves on some varities. The stalk meets the bottom of the leaf just below the bottom of the "V" in the

leaf shape. Of course, there are always exceptions to this. Ex: Alocasia Tigrina.

Soil conditions: Well drained, rich soil. Sun conditions: Part Shade, morning sun is perfect.

Colocasia

Colocasia Elephant Ears are the ones that have given ALL Elephant Ears a bad name. Here, my gardening friends, are the runners. Runners can be upto 6 feet away from the parent plant. But wait, this family has some georgous Elephant Ears. This variety would be more controlled if grown in a large container. Two of the most common are Black Magic and Imperial Taro.

This variety offers the widest range of colors. Stalks can be wine, black, green or cherry red. The stalk color can also be the

In Full

color of veining running through the leaf. Leaves are much waxier than the other families.

Colocasia stalk meets the bottom of the leaf almost in middle of the leaf shape. Each leaf will have a different colored dot on the top of the leaf exactly where the stalk meets the bottom. Of course, there are exceptions to this thought too. Ex: *Colocasia illustris* aka Imperial Taro.

Soil conditions: Well drained, rich soil. Wet, the wetter, the better. Can be grown in the garden, as a bog plant or even as an aquatic. Sun conditions: Shade, Sun, you name it... Typically, the less sun provided, the smaller the plant will remain.

Xanthosoma

Xanthosoma is the smallest of the Elephant Ear family. However, one of the most common giant Elephant Ears is in this family, *X. sagittifolium*. Xanthosomas do spread, but only about 10 inches from the parent plant.

This variety offers the most character in leaves. They have strange and bazarre growth habits. Ex: *X. atrovirens...* aka Mickey Mouse Taro forms a tiny vase with a long whisker at the tip of each leaf that holds water. It offers variegated foliage and stalks. Ex: *X. jacqinii lineatum*, the top layer of the leaf splits way from the bottom layer of the leaf.

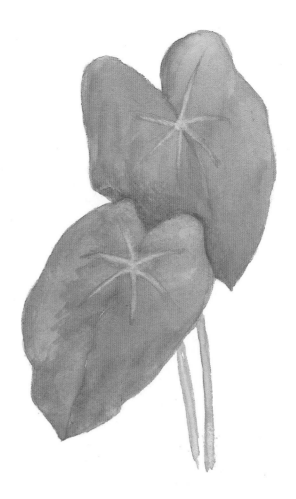

The top layer forms ripples and puckers that hold drops of water. The top layer and bottom layer are different colors, giving a variegated leaf.

Xanthosoma stalks meet the bottom of the leaf on the very edge of the "V" in the leaf shape. Another exclusive charateristic is that each leaf has a vein that runs along the edge of the leaf leaving about a 1/4 inch margin.

Soil conditions: Well drained, rich soil. Wet, the wetter, the better. Can be grown in the garden, as a bog plant or even as an aquatic. Sun conditions: Partial sun to full sun.

Biography: Virginia Boehme

I never had an interest in plants or gardening when I was younger. My world was all about.....well, me. That is until my 3 little men came along. Twin boys first and another boy 2 years later. I never could find a day care that met mommy's approval, so my husband and I decided for me to become a stay-at-home mom.

Now that we had become officially broke, I was a new mom within a very short period of time, I needed a sanctuary just for me. While inside, as my little men were playing, I played too. While they were sleeping, I usually cleaned. When they went outside to play, I found an undeniable attraction to my husband's shovel. As my little men grew and outside time became longer and more frequent, I became a digging fanatic. I explained to my little men that the yard was their area to play and the gardens were mommy's area to play. And play I did!

I discovered plant trading garden forums on the internet and quickly became known as DirtyFingernails. I traded plants out of my garden with people all over the world for something out of their garden. This allowed me an inexpensive opportunity to fill my gardens with rare and unusual plants. Plants that were not available in our area, but surprisingly grew to become happy plants.

My husband is the one that became infatuated with orchids. He has the need to own every single one, and I mean it! Since I always grew beautiful gardens with exotic plants, I had to incorporate orchids into my love of plants.....for the love of my husband. He, and sometimes we, acquired approximately 500 orchids within a 3 year period. I pretty much had a crash course in raising orchids. We began exhibiting our orchids against other orchid growers for competition.

Participating in these competitions inspired me to establish Fairie Tale Orchids. The goal was to make unusual orchids available to people that might not have the opportunity to visit an Orchid Show. In March 2007, I exhibited an orchid and it was awarded an Award of Merit from the American Orchid Society at the Jefferson Orchid Society show in Metairie, Louisiana. I named the orchid 'Lacey's Surprise'. It's exciting to have Fairie Tale Orchids officially recognized by the American Orchid Society....even if they don't know who "I" am.

Gardening Motto: Happiness is a shovel under my foot.

Favorite question when a gardener came to visit: Can I have a piece of that?

Gingers

Gingers Are Great Foliage Plants.

By Virginia Boehme, Fairie Tale Orchids

Gingers are great foliage plants, allowing the garden to incorporate different heights, shapes, colors and textures. There are varieties that thrive in full shade (Globba, Kaempferia), part shade (Hedychium, Curcuma, Alpinia), and full sun (Costus). Some are hardy to zone 7, while others may only be hardy in zone 10.

Several varieties: Globba, Kaempferia, Costus, Hedychium, Zingiber, Curcuma, Alpinia and more.

Hedychiums

Hedychiums give you a tall, dark green and variegated canes that begin to grow in early Spring. By mid Summer, Hedychiums begin to bloom on top of each cane. Bracts can grow to be 4 to 10 inches tall, giving way to beautiful flowers of various shades of yellows, whites, and oranges. Some blooms are a single color, while others are two-tones. The sepals are often a contrasting color, making the flower appear to be reaching for your attention. All are fragrant, each having it's own unique aroma. Each bract will produce a second set of blooms, some even three.

Hummingbirds enjoy visiting all colors of Hedychiums. Since the canes are tall, you get to enjoy the hummers high in the garden.

Canes can average 4'to 10' tall.

Hedychiums are hardy to zones 8 and 9. Grown in rich soil with good drainage. Sun conditions: Partial sun. Water during drought periods, but not really necessary. I often don't have time to water. They will continue to produce new canes throughout the growing season that will bloom until the first frost. Propagation is by division, however, the greenii variety will produce pups with air roots on the spent bract that can be planted.

Tip:

1. Plant rhyzome slightly above the soil, with roots planted deep, as you would plant an iris.

2. Leaves grow in only two directions while cane is maturing. When you see the top leaf growing in a third direction, you know the cane is about to bloom.

Costus

Costus are also known as Spiral Ginger. The canes grow tall and begin to take on a spiril pattern as it matures. Costus offer a wide range of foliages, making this variety a favorite in many gardens. They begin to grow in early Spring. By early Summer, the bract, resem-bling a tight pinecone, will appear at the top of the mature cane. Bract colors can be green, burgandy, pink, red, or orange.and grow to be 2 - 6 inches tall. Flowers are commonly a contrasting color of pink, white, orange, or yellow. Flowers usually only last 1 to 2 days, but the bract will continuously produce new flowers each day for weeks. Canes can average 3' to 8' tall.

Hummingbirds feed on every color of Costus bloom.

Costus are hardy to zones 8, 9 and 10. Grow in rich soil with good drainage.Sun conditions: Part Sun/Full Sun. Water during drought periods. They will produce new canes until the first frost. Propigation is by division or cuttings.

Tip:

1. The foliage only grows up one side of the cane, but because of the spiral growth habit it appears to grow on all sides of the cane.

2. As the cane grows, the leaves get bigger. As the cane matures and it is almost ready to bloom, the leaves begin getting smaller.

3. Propigate 6" to 8" cuttings in a gallon pot. No roottome need-ed! Over time, the cutting will appear to be dead, but it's not. The new growth will appear from the cutting just below the soil surface.

Globba

Globba gingers are also known as Dancing Ladies. They begin to grow in late Spring. By mid-Summer, the cane is mature and ready to bloom. Bracts can grow to be 6 to 9 inches long and are commonly pendulous, however, there are a few varities with erect bracts. Bract colors are usually green, yellow, red, purple and mauve. Flowers are yellow. They spike last for well over a month and are georgous as cut flowers. Canes can grow to 1' to 3' tall.

Globba gingers are hardy to zones 8 and 9. Grow in rich soil with good drainage. Sun conditions: Full Shade. Water during drought periods. New canes will continue to grow and bloom until the first frost. Propigation is by division. Some varities can be propigated by seed.

Kaempferia

Kaempferia gingers are also known as Peacock Gingers. They have very colorful leaves of greens, wines and silver. Most are low growing and multiply quickly. They bloom after the foliage is mature, continuing to bloom until the 1st frost. However, a few grow to be around 2' tall. The tall growing varieties multiply slower. They bloom prior to the foliage.

When foliage begins to appear, blooming is finished. The foliage will remain ntil the 1st frost. Kaempferias are hardy to zones 8 and 9. Grow in rich soil with good drainage. Sun conditions: Full Shade. Water during drought periods. Propagation is by division.

Curcuma

Curcuma gingers offer a tall foliage that can range from 2'to 8' tall. Foliages can be solid green, variegated with white or wine. Most bloom after the foliage is mature. However, there are a few varieties that bloom prior to the foliage. Blooms can last for 5 to 6 weeks on the plant or about 2 weeks as a cut flower. Bracts can range in colors of green, white, red, range, pink and even a blue.

Curcumas are hardy to zone 7 and 8. Grow in rich soil with good drainage.

Sun conditions: Shade to Part Sun. Water during drought periods. New plants will continue to grow. If they have time to mature, they may bloom prior to the first frost. Propagation is by division.

Zingiber

Zingiber gingers are also known as Pinecone Gingers or Shampoo Gingers. Foliages can be solid green, varietaged with white, cream or wine. Canes grow to be 4' to 8' tall. The bloom appears beside the cane and can be 1' to 3' tall. Bracts colors can be green, red, white, pink, orange or wine, and range in sizes of 5"to 12" tall. Flowers are usually white, cream or pink.

Bloom can last 4 to 6 weeks on the plant or about 2 weeks as a cut flower.

Zingibers are hardy to zones 8 through 10. Higher zone Zingibers should be lifted from soil and stored for the winter. Replant in Spring after threat of frost is over. Grow in rich soil with good drainage. Sun conditions: Full sun. Water during drought periods. New canes will continue to grow until the first frost. Propagation is by division.

Alpinia

Alpinia gingers offer tall canes of green or variegated leaves. Blooms are at the tip of each cane. Bracts can be erect cone shapes or long pendulous sprays. Bracts can come in colors of green. Blooms can range in colors of pink, white, cream, and red.

Alpinias are hardy to zones 8 through 10. Grow in rich soil with good drainage. Sun conditions: Part to Full Sun. Water during drought periods. Propagation is by division.

Tip: Alpinias bloom on the 2nd year canes. If allowed to go dormant after the 1st year, plant usually will not bloom. If blooms are desired, you must be protected from going dormant. Otherwise, it is simply used as a foliage plant.

Biography: Virginia Boehme

I never had an interest in plants or gardening when I was younger. My world was all about.....well, me. That is until my 3 little men came along. Twin boys first and another boy 2 years later. I never could find a day care that met mommy's approval, so my husband and I decided for me to become a stay-at-home mom.

Now that we had become officially broke, I was a new mom within a very short period of time, I needed a sanctuary just for me. While inside, as my little men were playing, I played too. While they were sleeping, I usually cleaned. When they went outside to play, I found an undeniable attraction to my husband's shovel. As my little men grew and outside time became longer and more frequent, I became a digging fanatic. I explained to my little men that the yard was their area to play and the gardens were mommy's area to play. And play I did!

I discovered plant trading garden forums on the internet and quickly became known as DirtyFingernails. I traded plants out of my garden with people all over the world for some-

Above: *White Gingers* by Betty Gay.

thing out of their garden. This allowed me an inexpensive opportunity to fill my gardens with rare and unusual plants. Plants that were not available in our area, but surprisingly grew to become happy plants.

My husband is the one that became infatuated with orchids. He has the need to own every single one, and I mean it! Since I always grew beautiful gardens with exotic plants, I had to incorporate orchids into my love of plants.....for the love of my husband. He, and sometimes we, acquired approximately 500 orchids within a 3 year period. I pretty much had a crash course in raising orchids. We began exhibiting our orchids against other orchid growers for competition.

Participating in these competitions inspired me to establish Fairie Tale Orchids. The goal was to make unusual orchids available to people that might not have the opportunity to visit an Orchid Show. In March 2007, I exhibited an orchid and it was awarded an Award of Merit from the American Orchid Society at the Jefferson Orchid Society show in Metairie, Louisiana. I named the orchid 'Lacey's Surprise'. It's exciting to have Fairie Tale Orchids officially recognized by the American Orchid Society....even if they don't know who "I" am.

Gardening Motto: Happiness is a shovel under my foot.

Favorite question when a gardener came to visit: Can I have a piece of that?

Purple Passionflower vines, passiflora incarnata, make fine summer hedges or screens. The flowers are incredible!phere in shady natural areas.

Climbing Plants

Our native Muscadine, Vitis rotundifolia, can be trained to behave on a trellis or fence. Fruits have been a southern favorite for generations.

Climbers Are Attractive Features in Most Established Gulf Coast Gardens.

By Lois Boykin and Judy Lucci

They are especially well suited to enhance attractive features and to conceal, mask unattractive views, or separate yard areas into "garden rooms." Arbors or lattice panels are traditional architectural elements used to support climbers. Stair and deck railings are frequently used to support evergreens and flowing vines, frequently growing in pots selected to harmonize with over-all garden settings.

Lamp posts provide an excellent place to display a carefully .tended blooming or evergreen climber. Once established, perennial climbers provide easy care beauty in the garden year after year.

One of the oldest and most often grown vines in the Southern garden is the Wisteria. It is a member of the Pea Family, *Fabaceae*, and was named in honor of Caspar Wistar, (1761-1818) an anatomy professor at the University of Pennsylvania.

Wisterias are vigorous vines that are sometime hard to keep under control. They are hardy, high climbing and will live to become twisted woody trunks several inches in diameter. They have many landscape uses. They grow best on trellises, wires, arbors and pergo-las. They can even be trimmed to remain self –standing trees or espaliered on a wall.

The Chinese wisteria (*Wisteria sinensis*) is the most popular plant due to its flowering habit. It can grow to a height of 25 plus feet with flower clusters 6 to 12 inches long that appear before the foliage has expanded. The flowers are a showy violet-blue and fragrant, blooming all at once, after frost in the early spring. There is also a white flowering form of Chinese wisteria (*w. sinenis*) which is very fragrant. The Japanese wisteria (*Wisteria floribunda*) will also reach a height of 25 plus feet, blooms of purple open as the foliage is expanding. These flower clusters will reach 12 to 18 inches long and are very fragrant. This species may bloom a little later than the Chinese wisteria. There are also varieties of the Japanese Wisteria that have blooms of different colors; Alba- white, Carnea-light pink, Macrobtrys'- reddish-violet.

In order for wisteria to bloom well, it must have six or more hours of full sun, a deep moderate fertile moist soil that does not dry out excessively. Mulch the base well, watch it grow and enjoy!

ꜛ A local favorite is the Fig Vine (*ficus pumila*). Although Fig Vines need to be trimmed to be kept under control it will attach itself to wood, masonry and even metal. This evergreen is an aggressive vine capable of entirely covering a large area in a single season. Young fig vines are susceptible to mild Gulf Coast frost but once established, they will withstand frost as low as 15-20 degrees

The young leaves are tiny, delicate and heart shaped but as is grows, the foliage ultimately develops into large leathery leaves on stubby branches that will also bear large oblong fruit. Do not use on wood as it traps moisture and encourages rot.

ꜛ The Clematis (*clematis intergiflora*) is a perennial hybrid propagated to do well on the Gulf Coast. They are aggressive but controllable engineered to provide abundant blooms in a wide variety of colors from early spring through mid summer. Plant Clematis to grow on arbors and trellises in rich, loose, fast-draining soil. To keep the roots cool, mulch or place a flat rock over the soil or plant a shallow rooted ground cover. The tops of the vine like to be in the sun. Tie up tender vines as they are easily broken. Apply a complete liquid fertilizer monthly during the growing season. The showy flowers are followed by fluffy clusters of seeds with tails. Clematis will die back after a frost. Wait until spring to prune and vines will again cover in no time.

Wisteria illustration by Louise Estes.

⌐ Though not winter hardy here, there are three tropical climbers that are very popular. The Alamanda (*Alamanda cathartica*) and the Mandevilla (*Mandevilla sanderi*) are both rapid growers requiring little or no care that produce abundant showy yellow or pink flowers. Both plants are ideally suited for climbing on fences, light post and trellises. Plants will do well either in sun to partial shade.

⌐ The Bougainvilla (*bougainvillea*) is less seen but is an extravagant bloomer in a wide variety of colors. It is susceptible to frost but can be grown in protected pots if covered during frost.

Other climbers that are consistently successful and trouble free in our gardens are:

⌐ Major Wheeler Honeysuckle: (*Lonicera sempervirens*) Red and gold blooms that appear all summer and into fall.

⌐ Trumpet Vines: (*Campsis tagliabauna*) Fast growing and easy to grow. A wide range of colors from red to orange that attracts hummingbirds!

⌐ Scotch Ivy: (*Araliaceae*) An aggressive climber that is great for covering brick or stucco walls.

⌐ English Ivy: (*Hedera helix*) Not an aggressive climber but used extensively as ground in shady garden areas.

⌐ While not members of the true tropical Jasmine family; Carolina Yellow, Confederate Yellow and Star White jasmines are a frequently used vine in our gardens. All three bloom profusely in the early spring. Star Jasmine stays in bloom as long as two weeks and has an intense fragrant scent. The Oriental or Asiatic Jasmine is an evergreen ground creeper widely used very effectively as a low maintenance ground cover. It does not climb nor does it bloom.

Chinese Wisteria, *Wisteria sinensis*, artfully trained above garage doors.

Vegetables

Illustrations by Louise Estes.

Vegetable Gardening on the Gulf Coast of Alabama Is Fun, Relaxing, Enjoyable and Delicious.

By Jack W. Boykin

This humble process of planting seed and plants into the soil ties each of us with the ancient order of mankind to provide an ordered and predictable way for the energy of the sun to be made available for our bodies.

Plants are that portion of the earth's life form that chose to carry out their biological functions in one fixed location and to move about the earth through their seeds or roots. Therefore the condition of the soil as well as the air and light above the soil are the control factors by which a plant reaches its maximum growth and reproductive potential.

For vegetable gardening to be fun, relaxing and enjoyable the garden must be of a size that you can easily care for. Whether it is a 5 gallon pot planted with tomatoes and lettuce or a multi row garden in the back yard; it is important to plant only as many seeds or plants as you have time to care for.

Plants are principally composed of carbon, nitrogen, hydrogen, oxygen and minerals. Just like the human body. The oxygen, carbon, hydrogen are principally ingested from the air. The minerals are principally ingested from the soil. Nitrogen may be ingested from both soil and air. So as a gardener it is important that you ensure that the soil is of a texture to allow air and water to migrate easily to the roots.

Plants of course need sunlight since the DNA of the plant sets up a self-regulating and self-reproductive biochemical reaction system to receive the energy of sunlight and convert the sun light and carbon dioxide to sugars, carbohydrates, cellulose and a whole host of chemical compounds which create each of the particular vegetables you are planting. For the most part all vegetables require six to eight hours of direct sunlight during the day. During the heat of the summer (July and August) the tender plants such as lettuce, greens and tomatoes may require some shading. This subject will be address with each item to follow.

In addition to water, minerals and air, the temperature of the soil and air are a major factor for proper plant growth. The biochemical reactions which start the germination and growth process are temperature dependent and will not properly occur until the activation temperature for each step of the plant growth cycle is met. Insure that the soil temperature is above the minimum required before the seed and hot house plants are set in the garden.

Asparagus

The ancient Egyptians considered this plant a delicacy and we along the Gulf Coast share with them the culinary delicacy. Growing

asparagus requires some gardening adaptations due to the high temperature and almost year round growing season. Plant the asparagus crown 8-10 inches deep in a two to three foot wide row. The row bottom should be fertilized with 10-20-10 fertilizer at a rate of ? pound per 100ft. Cover the crown with two to four inches of compost or light soil and water. After the crowns have sprouted to a six inch height add another 2 to 3 inches of compost or soil for the first year's growth. Each year thereafter add additional 2-3 inches of compost with ammonium nitrate added at ? pound per 100 feet. It is important that the pH (acidity) of the asparagus bed be maintained at 6.0 to 7.3 to ensure healthy growth. Also the harvesting season should be limited to 5-6 weeks each spring.

Beans

Essentially every type of bean grows bountifully in our area. String beans, butter beans, snap beans, dry beans all these members of the legume family flourish along the Alabama Gulf Coast.

Soil types may vary from dense to light or organic soils. Always incorporate decomposed hay, straw or leaves into the soil for maximum growth and productivity. The roots need access to as much air as possible to generate the beans own nitrogen. Try to keep the soil between 6-7.5 pH. If too low add lime, if too high add iron sulfate. Make sure the

soil at planting depth is above 60F preferably 65F. Along the Gulf Coast this usually means April – May planting. Planting a few beans every two weeks throughout spring and summer can ensure a full and late season supply until December.

Control of virus with sprays of wettable sulfur every two weeks and control crawling or flying insects with vinegar and hot pepper sprays. This will usually suffice to allow a substantial crop to develop for each planting.

Beets

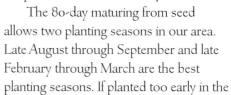
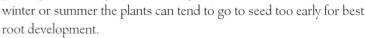

Beets produce best when grown in deeply tilled and organically mulched soils. Beets are at their best flavor when allowed to mature to a fully leafed plant at temperatures between 60 to 70F.

The 80-day maturing from seed allows two planting seasons in our area. Late August through September and late February through March are the best planting seasons. If planted too early in the winter or summer the plants can tend to go to seed too early for best root development.

Plant small amounts of beets every two weeks and ensure adequate spoil moisture to prevent the slightly bitter taste that occurs if the roots mature on dry soil.

To get the best seed germination, soak the seed in water for 24 hours before planting. Also cover the planted seeds with compost or commercial planting soil mixture to ensure no soil crusting above the seeds until the plants are fully leafed. After the beet plants are 3 to 4 inches high trim them to one plant every three to four inches; between 6-8 inch plant height, fertilize with high nitrogen fertilizer and mulch around the plant row to retain moisture.

Broccoli, Brussel Sprouts and Cabbage

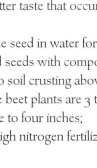

The crucifer families of plants grow best when the weather is a 45 to 75 degrees air temperature. Therefore along the Alabama

Gulf Coast, this is from October to March. During midwinter when the one to two weeks of night time temperatures below 40F it is advisable to cover the plants with a light cloth.

It is important that these plants grow vigorously during the early stage of development. Well prepared light organic soil, adequate fertilizer and adequate moisture with a pH between 6.0-7.5 will ensure rapid growth.

Due to the short cool season in our spring it is best to plant transplants in late January or early February. In the fall seed may be planted in September. Separate rows by 12 inches and plants by 12-16 inches.

The principle cool weather pests are cabbage lopers which can be controlled by hot pepper spray or natural pyrithium.

Melons, Cantaloupe, Watermelon and Honeydew

Melons should be planted in sandy organic soil which will allow a deep and rapidly expanding root system. The soil temperature should be above 60F. Fall and spring crops are usually successful. Fall crops are usually seed planted in late August. Spring crops are usually planted in late February or March. Some cool weather cover is advisable. For cool soil planting use "hot caps" over each plant until soil temperature is above 60F.

Melons require substantial amounts of fertilizer. Ensure the application if fertilizer every two weeks until the melon growth is complete.

Carrots

To grow carrots properly in this area, you must ensure proper soil, light, moisture, spacing and air temperature.

Deep (8" to 12") turned, soft organic sandy soil with lightly pre mixed fertilizer. The temperature for growth should be between 40 to 80F. After thinning the carrots to 3 to 4 inch intervals, side-dress the row with high nitrogen fertilizer and mulch.

Cucumber

Cucumbers require 8 to 10 inch deep light loam soil. Annual infusions of organic matter (2-4 inches per year) are needed to ensure the rapid growth of roots. Fertilize heavily and ensure good soil moisture throughout the entire growing season. Low nitrogen with high potassium and phosphate fertilizer is preferred.

Early Fall planting (September) and mid Spring planting are usually the best time to produce excellent crops. Use of "hot caps" or row covers can be used in early March to obtain the longest time of productivity for the spring crop. The objective of using the covers is to protect the plant until the nighttime temperature is over 60 F.

Corn

For the home gardener along the Alabama coast there are two main varieties—Silver Queen and Silver King—corn. Both grow abundantly well as long as the basic preparation is made.

Adjust the pH of high organic content soil to between 6 to 7. Use low nitrogen, high mineral fertilizer (10-20-20). After the stalks reach 12-14 inches mulch with hay, straw or leaves to maintain root moisture.

For home grown sweet corn, it is best to plant in 5 feet by 5 feet squares at 1 foot intervals between seed. This will provide 25 stalks and up to 50 ears. Plant these squares of corn at 2 to 4 week intervals to ensure sweet corn from early spring until frost. Corn can be planted as early as late January until September.

Egg Plant

Egg plants are of tropical origin and require warm weather to grow properly. Night time temperature of 60 F are required for the plant to grow properly. Therefore it is best to set out transplants when the nights warm to 60 F.

The intense sun and temperature of the latter half of July until mid August can cause the crop to have a slightly bitter taste. It is best to slightly shade the plants during this time. The plants will continue to produce until frost. If you plant a fall crop, transplants should be set out in August to allow fruit production before 50?F nights occur.

Lettuce

Lettuce can be grown year round along the Gulf Coast. When the frost or freeze weather occurs small areas of lettuce can be covered by a protective enclosure with a light bulb or kerosene lamp.

For the home gardener a two foot by two foot square of lettuce will produce more product than several families would normally eat. This style planting allows for easy frost and heat protection and for the all important moisture control. Do not let the top 1 inche of soil become dry. Keep it at moderate moisture level. Mulch rows with compost or grass to conserve moisture and reduce weeds.

Transplanting lettuce is the most effective way to get the best productivity from seeds and to control placement in the garden. Four to six inch tall transplants do well any time of year as long as they are kept moist and protected from weather extremes throughout the year. When the transplant are well established (2-3 weeks after transplant) side dress with high nitrogen fertilizer (ammonium sulfate).

Onions

Along the Gulf Coast of Alabama the interval of daily sunshine is about 10-12 hours per day. You must choose an onion that will develop bulbs in that interval of light. Make sure the onion plants you purchase are the "short day" variety.

Onion transplants should be planted in late January and early February. The soil pH should be between 6 to 7. The soil should be tilled with compost to at least 6 inches of depth. Mix in a low nitrogen fertilizer (8-10-10) and ensure the soil is moist at the time of setting out transplants.

Transplants should be set out about 4 inches apart in rows of approximately 16 inch separation. Once the planting shows new growth side dress with Ammonium sulfate. Adequate moisture is required throughout the life cycle of the onion plant. This is especially so while the bulb is enlarging. All of the food for this bulb growth carries from the above ground foliage. By ensuring maximum moisture and nutrients for the onion foliage you will ensure the maximum bulb size.

Peas

This article is about African style field peas (black eyes, creamers, croweders, etc.) They require minimal fertilizer but do well with modest amounts of compost mixed in. Try to keep the soil pH between 6 to 7. Plant at 4-8 inches in the spring at 16 inch rows.

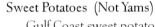

Since the progenerator of these crops originated in the tropics, it is necessary to let the soil temperature reach at least 60 F at planting depth before planting otherwise germinations will be poor and damping off for the growing plants will occur. May is the best month to plant and plantings may continue until September.

After the first harvest from your peas, side dress with ammonium sulfate or nitrate for future production.

Spinach

Spinach requires a near neutral pH soil. It is shallow rooted and grows best in mild to cool temperatures. As a result the soil pH should be lined to 6.5 to 7.5 and infused with compost to produce a light loam soil.

For the gardener a two foot by two foot square of spinach plants can feed a family well for several weeks. Therefore it is best to plant succession "squares" of spinach at one month intervals throughout the year. Follow the seed company recommendations for the best variety depending on the time and temperature. "Bloomsdale" and "American" variety do well in the spring. Fall planting should occur only after soil temperature drops below 70 F. Transplants may be a better choice for fall gardeners.

Soaking seeds in a jar of water for up to two days in the refrigerator will help the seeds to germinate faster. A teaspoon of vinegar in a quart of water containing the seeds will ensure a softening of the seed shells and faster germination.

Squash/Zucchini

These plants should be grown in rows three feet apart and two feet separation in each row. The soil is best as a sandy loam with large amount of compost infused into the soil to keep the soil at 6-7.5 ph by the use of lime and side dress with a low nitrogen fertilizer (8-10-10).

Make sure the soil temperature is above 65 F in the spring. Successful planting may be continued until 120 days before frost. Soil moisture is very important during the time of germination for seeds as well as the growing season.

The squash plant should be watered from the ground up. A small trench around the plant will allow the roots to be watered without wetting the leaves. It is best to leave the leaves and blossoms dry to avoid fungus growth.

Sweet Potatoes (Not Yams)

Gulf Coast sweet potatoes grow best in a heavy loam soil with good drainage. They need a slightly acidic soil with ph between 5.5 - 6.5. Plenty of water—although they are drought tolerant. Do not over fertilize. When it is needed fertilize with low nitrogen, higher potassium and phosphate fertilizers. Bone meal and potassium nitrate (KNO_3) and potassium sulfate (K_2SO_4) are excellent for nutrient rich potatoes.

Soil temperature should be at least 65 F before planting. This is usually the months of May along the Gulf Coast of Alabama. Plant the sweet potatoes three to four leaves deep in moist soil and keep soil most until rain or the plants show vigorous growth. Before runners start to cover the planted bed, side dress the sweet potatoes with low nitrogen fertilizer. Crops are usually ready for harvest in approximately 100 days after the slips are planted. Be sure you harvest before "frost" so that the root will be in storage about 50 F. Let the roots dry between layers of cardboard or paper in a warm area for a few (2-4) weeks to gain the best sweet flavor. Then keep cool and enjoy as you wish.

Tomatoes

What else can be written about tomatoes? Plant the vine. Keep it moist. Fertilize weekly. Spray every two weeks with pyrithrium and copper sulfate. Make sure the soil has plenty of lime and spray leaves with calcium chloride solutions. Then you will have tomatoes—all you can eat.

There are a few tricks of the trade to allow you to grow "bragging" tomatoes.

Set out transplants in late February and cover then with "hot caps" or clear plastic covers to ensure best warming of plant and soil for the spring growth. Make sure the plants are not exposed to wind or cold at night temperatures. In the fall use the opposite procedures and cover the plants when night time temperatures drop below 75.

Set out transplants in early September. Keep soil moist but not too wet.

Set the transplant root ball approximately 6 inches below top of soil and place a one quart milk container or clay pot within 6" of the root. The container top is to be ground level and with a hole in the bottom to deep water the roots.

Once growth starts fertilize every two weeks throughout the fruiting season.

Turnip & Rutabaga

Turnips and rutabagas are cool weather crops and should be planted in weather above 35 and below85 degrees. The best time of year to plant these crops is in late September through February.

Soil pH needs to be 6.0 to 7.5 and not too much fertilizer. Sandy loan with incorporated compost is usually adequate to grow these crops. If fertilizer is needed use a low nitrogen fertilizer as a row side dress after the plants are above six inches tall.

Space the plants (thin out) the seedlings to about four inches apart in rows about 12 inches apart for turnips. For rutabaga plants space about 8 to 10 inches apart and rows at 16 to 20 inches apart.

Rutabaga requires an extra 40 to 60 days of growth past the time of turnips. As a result they should be planted at least 4 months before expected 85 degree daytime weather. This is usually a January planting along the Gulf Coast.

Potatoes

Along the Gulf Coast of Alabama "red skin" potatoes are by far the most popular; although other varieties are often grown. The la Soda and Pontiac are the most often grown in the coastal region.

These potatoes can literally be grown lying on top of the ground. The pieces of seed potatoes can be placed on a 4-6 inch layer of grass compost and covered with a foot of hay or straw. Plenty of 10-10-10 fertilizing materials in first top cover and a fine potatoes crop can be made. The more conventional furrow of 6 inch deep planting in the rich compost soil is often preferred.

Potatoes are a cool weather crop and prefer 40 to 80?F weather. An early February planting and a May harvest is the most common growing season. Fall planting in early September can produce a December harvest crop.

Fertilize the soil or mulch bed heavily before planting. There should not be a need to fertilize after planting. Keep the soil moist but not excessively wet.

Peppers

Peppers require warm weather, lots of sun, plenty of fertilizer and water, and an optimum pH of 6-7. Planting in a raised row with a furrow on each side of the planted row is useful to ensure moist but drained soil around the pepper plant roots. Ground covers are often used around pepper plants to keep the roots warm during early season planting. Space the plant about 16 inches apart and in 16-20 inch rows.

Biography: Jack W. Boykin

I was raised in central Alabama in a family which always had a vegetable garden. In my first grade year in school I was assigned a 10 foot by 10 foot garden to grow whatever I chose. Over those years in school my greatest achievement was a 30lb black diamond watermelon.

Throughout my years at Auburn University I grew a few vegetables in large potted plants. My vegetable achievement was the fermented remains of corn and potatoes mixed with the syrups from peach and pair cans left at Mrs. McGar's boarding house where I lived and worked. My having access to the proper equipment from the chemical engineering labs allowed me to share the distilled vapors from my corn and potato crops, after the fall football games with the boarding house residents.

As my wife Lois and I moved around the country we always planted a vegetable garden. As I traveled to build chemical plants around the world I planted seeds at every industrial site over the forty years. My Aunt Ludie's "rattle snake" green beans in three sites in China, watermelons in Greece, field peas in South America, etc.

Today I am fortunately relegated to a 30 by 70 foot fifteen row raised bed garden in the Village of Montrose, in Baldwin County.

There my neighbors delightfully accept each of the variety of vegetables discussed in this book.

John and Jane always give me a Christmas package with the seeds of vegetables they prefer. Their favorite is broccoli and brussell sprouts. Buck and Virginia politely call and remind me if I forgot their monthly vegetable basket. They prefer turnips and cauliflower. Jim and Annette prefer the cabbage and rattle snake string beans. Our friend Linda has been so kind as to never refuse to accept a grocery bag of whatever is being harvested at the time when she visits Lois.

What a great joy to be able to share the sun light converted by the DNA of plants to vegetables with such a wonderful fraternity and be a part of the eternity of light and life. — Jack W. Boykin, Montrose Gardener, Baldwin County, Alabama

Fruit Trees

Successful Fruit Plants for Coastal Alabama

Text and photos by
Monte L. Nesbitt, Horticulturist, Auburn University

The abundant rainfall, long growing season, mild winters and rich soils found near Mobile Bay make it possible to grow many types of fruit plants. The popular fruits in our diet are from very diverse families of plants, some of which have climatic requirements not found in coastal Alabama. The number of chill hours accumulated in winter and early spring is important in selecting the right fruit plants to grow here. The Eastern Shore area commonly gets approximately 400 to 500 hours of chilling each year, but may sometimes get less than 350 or more than 900 hours. Deciduous fruit varieties that don't get adequate chilling may produce few if any fruits. Many varieties of deciduous fruits, including apples, pears, peaches, and walnuts have too high chill requirement to be grown successfully on the Gulf Coast. Additionally, some fruit varieties may bloom too early in the Spring and get frozen as a rule, because the hours of warm temperature they need to commence growth and flowering is low. The Gulf Coast often experiences extended warm periods during the months of January, February and March, which increases freeze risk for some fruits, like plums.

Certain subtropical fruits, including citrus, can be grown on the Gulf Coast, and don't have chill hour limitations. However, freeze hardiness is usually not as great in evergreen subtropicals as it is in deciduous plants that lose their leaves and go dormant, so some protection of the plants during winter freezes may be required.

Baldwin and Mobile Counties falls into USDA hardiness zone 8b, having an average low temperature of 15 F to 20 F, which is cold enough to kill all mainstream citrus fruits and other subtropical plants. Subtropical and tropical fruits must also mature their fruit before the onset of freezing, winter temperatures. Bananas, for example, can survive some winters in coastal Alabama, but the fruit takes 11 months or more to mature, making it near impossible to produce banana fruit successfully outdoors, because of the likelihood of a fruit-injuring frost or freeze.

The high rainfall and humidity, coupled with warm temperatures creates a favorable climate for insects and diseases on many fruits. While some diseases, like Brown Rot of peaches, can be managed through dedication to spraying with fungicides, others such as Pierce's Disease on vinifera (bunch-type) grapes have no known cure, practically guaranteeing that the plants will die in a short span of time. The following list of fruit plants is composed of those that do well in terms of winter chilling satisfaction, spring freeze risk, freeze hardiness, soil adaptation and limiting pests.

Blueberry

The rabbiteye blueberry (*Vaccinium ashei*) is well adapted to the Gulf Coast, being native to the southern U.S. Rabbiteye blueberry fruit is nice sized and wonderful tasting. Although late spring frosts sometimes damage flowers, fruit production is usually reliable if plants are kept in good health and pruned regularly. The key to success is to set plants in soil that is acidic (4.5 to 5.2), and to use low rates of fertilizer containing ammonium or urea forms of nitrogen. Plants make a large shrub, and should be given eight to ten feet of space to spread, and be expected to grow to a height of six to ten feet. Several good varieties are found in the area, including 'Climax', 'Premier', and 'Tifblue'. It is important to plant more than one variety on a site for cross pollination.

Blackberry

Cultivated and improved blackberries are well adapted to the Gulf Coast climate, although some varieties are believed to have higher chill requirement than others. Blackberries may be trailing (run on the ground) or semi-erect in growth habit, so a simple trellis or fence to support them with and keep fruit off the ground is needed. Each year, new canes are produced that produce fruit one year later, and then die. So pruning of old, dead canes must be done each year. Several varieties of thorn-free blackberries are available, including 'Arapaho', 'Navaho' and 'Apache'. The thorn-free varieties are productive, bearing fruit from late May to late July, but have problematic foliage and cane diseases that may difficult to control in the home landscape. Thorny varieties like 'Choctaw' and 'Kiowa' bear bigger fruit and more abundantly, but they also have a serious disease problem called Double Blosssom or Rosette, which deforms flowers and fruit and requires frequent fungicide sprays to control.

Muscadine Grapes

Muscadine grapes (*Vitis rotundifolia*) are native to the Southeastern U.S., and thus very adapted to grow here and bear fruit. These plants are commonly called "scuppernongs", which is a misnomer, since 'Scuppernong' is the name of one variety of muscadine. There are many different varieties of muscadines that can be grown on the Gulf Coast, producing bronze, red or black fruit over a harvest period of several weeks. Berries ripen individually within the cluster, rather than an entire cluster ripening at once. Two flowering types are available and must be understood. Self-fertile plants do not need a pollinator to bear fruit, but pistillate only (female) varieties must be planted near a self-fertile plant for adequate pollination. Muscadines grow vigorously, and will ramble out of control, without a trellis and pruning each winter. Plants need full sunlight, a 15 ft spacing between plants, fertilizer in spring, and soil pH adjusted to 6.0 to 6.5.

Persimmons

Native persimmons can be found growing wild in Baldwin and Mobile County. This local species, *Diospyrous virginiana*, makes a tall, often slender tree with small (golf-ball size) fruit that must ripen thoroughly to become non-astringent and edible. Oriental persimmons (*Diospyrous kaki*), although not native, grow well in Alabama and bear larger (tomato size) fruit, some of which is low in astringency and can be eaten while still firm. 'Fuyu' is one of the most popular, large-fruited, low astringency varieties. The trees grow slowly, ultimately attaining a height of 10-12 feet. Fruit ripens in the fall and early winter, often losing leaves as the fruit reaches peak color. Oriental persimmons have few pest problems, although some limb and bark canker problems have been observed where narrow branch angles are not pruned or corrected.

Pomegranate

Pomegranates (*Punica granata*) are grown throughout the U.S. and are adapted to grow on the Gulf Coast. Pomegranates, popular 30 to 40 years ago, are regaining their popularity, because of the high antioxidant values in the fruit. Pomegranates grow into a large dense shrub, and may be trained into a small tree. Fruit is large and attractive, showing color in mid to late summer. Fruit ripens in very late summer and early fall months. The standard variety, which is still most commonly found is called 'Wonderful', and more varieties are becoming available. They have no pollinator requirements, but need to be planted in full sun for maximum productivity.

Pecans

Pecans are grown all over Southwest Alabama, and many former pecan orchards in and around Daphne and Fairhope have become residential neighborhoods. Pecan trees have a very low chill requirement and are slow to bud out in the spring, making them a good fruit plant for South Alabama. Pecan trees need lots of space in the landscape. Trees can reach heights of 50-60 feet, and have similar limb spread. They are fast growing, and can add shade quickly to a new home landscape, but ideally should not be planted within falling distance of a house or structure. Older varieties that are found in many existing orchards and landscapes are disease susceptible and often fail to make good crops, except in unusually dry years. Newer varieties, such as 'Gafford', 'Kanza', 'Carter', and 'Syrup Mill' have much greater foliage and nut disease resistance, and stand a better chance of producing nice quality nuts when grown in a non-commercial set-

ting. Most pecan varieties need pollinator trees nearby to increase nut production. In most areas of coastal Alabama, there is adequate pecan pollen around to set fruit on a single tree in a landscape, but planting two varieties is recommended if space allows and gives more assurance of good pollination.

Figs

Figs (*Ficus carica*) are examples of fruit plants whose cold hardiness of 15-20oF, is right at the same average low temperatures found on the Alabama Gulf Coast. If normal to warmer-than normal winter temperatures are experienced, figs will grow in size and increase their bearing capability each year, ultimately becoming tall (10-12 ft) and spreading trees. If a hard freeze occurs, fig trees can be substantially killed back, especially those growing on colder than average "micro-sites". During warm periods, figs may need to be pruned each year to keep the tree's size manageable, and pruning is beneficial to fruit production. Figs need to be planted in full sun for best production. Low rates of fertilizer are recommended. Mulching is beneficial in helping figs cope with soil-borne nematodes that are a common problem. There are several varieties of figs that can be grown on the Gulf Coast, but the two most commonly preferred are 'Brown Turkey' and 'Celeste', the latter reported to have the best cold hardiness. Neither variety requires a pollinator.

Citrus

Citrus trees have varying degrees of cold hardiness, depending on the species and the rootstock that it may be grafted on. Limes, true lemons, and citrons are among the least cold hardy, and will suffer cold injury during mild freezes in the upper 20's. The intermediate category includes oranges, grapefruits, pummelos, and many mandarins (clementines, tangerines, tangelos) that can tolerate some mid to lower 20's (23-26 oF). The cold hardy group includes Satsuma mandarin that can survive to mid-teens, kumquats, which are slightly more cold hardy than Satsuma, citrangequats, Changsha tangerine, Yuzu, and certain other "less edible" fruits, such as Ichang lemon that can tolerate temperatures of 10-15 oF in some cases.

Trifoliate orange is a desired rootstock for citrus growing on the Gulf Coast in situ-

ations where no or minimal freeze protection will be provided. Trifoliate orange grows more slowly, keeps trees smaller and provides greater cold hardiness than any other rootstock, and should be requested when purchasing plants. A more dwarfing form of Trifoliate Orange, called 'Flying Dragon', is also a good choice for home citrus on the Eastern Shore. Plants on 'Flying Dragon' are more easily covered during freezes or kept in containers that can be moved to a protected location.

Satsumas are a good citrus plant for south Alabama, because the fruit ripens early for citrus (October-December) allowing better chance to harvest all the fruit before a fall freeze occurs. All citrus fruit freeze when air temperatures drop to 26-28 oF, so freeze damage to the fruit crop is a risk every year, especially to those types of citrus that don't fully ripen until December, January or later. There are four-six Satsuma varieties that can be planted, including 'Owari', 'Brown's Select' and 'Silverhill', which are mid to late ripening (October-November), and 'Armstrong Early', 'LA Early' and 'Early St. Ann', which are earlier ripening varieties, that can have ripe fruit in early October. The sweet kumquat 'Meiwa' and the sour kumquat 'Nagami' are excellent citrus plants to grow in the landscape, having a high degree of cold hardiness, nice tree form, and beautiful winter fruit.

Other popular citrus that do well in the area, albeit with greater freeze injury risk, include sweet oranges, such as 'Hamlin' 'Marr's Early', and 'Louisiana Sweet'; navel oranges, such as 'Washington' and 'Cara Cara', a red-fleshed navel; grapefruit, including 'Ruby Red', 'Rio Red' and others; and 'Meyer' lemon, which is a hybrid lemon that ripens fruit in the fall and takes more cold than other true lemons.

A common problem with citrus in coastal Alabama is inadequate fertilizer practices, resulting in poor winter survival and erratic cropping. Citrus should be fertilized in late February, late May and late June, with a complete fertilizer that includes minor nutrients. The amount of fertilizer to add depends on the nitrogen level in the analysis, and the age of the trees. Citrus trees on trifoliate orange rootstock need about 1/10 pound of actual nitrogen (one pound 10-10-10 fertilizer) per year of tree age, with a maximum of 1.5 lbs nitrogen (15 lbs, 10-10-10) per tree. The target rate of fertilizer is split evenly among the three application times listed (February, May, June). Other cultural recommendations for citrus include full sunlight when possible, although part shade is acceptable, and thorough watering during the bloom and post bloom periods (April to May).

Biography: Monte Nesbitt

Monte Nesbitt is a research associate and horticulturist with Auburn University's Department of Horticulture. He is located in Baldwin County at the Gulf Coast Research & Extension Center in Fairhope, AL, an 800 acre agricultural farm research center. Nesbitt studies some of the important fruit and nut crops grown in the coastal section of the state, including pecans, citrus, peaches, blackberries and others. Nesbitt, a native of Texas, has been working at the center, since 1994, after receiving a B.S. degree in Horticulture from Texas Tech University and an M.S. in Horticulture from Texas A&M University. The Auburn center at Fairhope currently has over 500 citrus trees planted, and holds a collection of 100 varieties of citrus, including 35 varieties of satsumas.

Herbs

Easy Tips on Growing, Pruning and Harvesting Herbs

By Joan M. Thorington

I choose the following three herbs: Italian Basil, Prostrate Rosemary, and Mint because of their abundance of uses in the kitchen, the simplicity of care and their performance in our coastal climate. The annual herb basil (*Ocymum basilicum*) is usually a plant that grows best in the cooler temperatures of spring and fall in our area. When someone mentions basil I automatically think of the fabulous flavor of a pesto sauce which is a superb topping on our locally caught seafood. Being an impatient gardener, I prefer to let someone else do the work of starting herbs from seed and just buy

mine ready to plant and eat. Basil should be harvested routinely before the stems go to seed (unless you collect seeds for the next planting season), and the stemmed plant can be stored in a jar with water inside of the refrigerator for a few days before use. Clip your basil stems from the outside edges of the plant almost at ground level. Early morning is the optimum time to harvest all of your

OCYMUM BASILICUM
BASIL

herbs to capture the natural oils and rinse any dirt off the leaves and place on paper towels to dry. Basil will perform better in your garden or container when severely pruned once a month during the summer growing season. I will offer tips on how to store and save dried herbs later in the article. In Italian history basil was associated with sympathy, compassion, love and devotion. Sixteenth century herbalists used basil on snake and scorpion bites.

The next on my list of favorite herbs is Rosemary. There are two types of rosemary that grow well in our area; the upright and my favorite, the prostrate or "creeping" variety because it is an excellent choice for container planting. This type of rosemary (*Rosmarinus prostrates*) works well in rock gardens because of its growth pattern, colorful blooms and not to mention the fabulous aroma when the breeze blows.

Creeping rosemary is very easy to grow and the variety "Tuscan Blue" is usually found in our local garden shops. Baldwin and Mobile Counties in Alabama are fortunate to have dedicated nurserymen and women who grow a large variety of herbs. Garden shops such as Preast's Petals & Pottery in Fairhope has one of the largest selections of these locally grown herbs for sale with a knowledgeable and courteous staff to assist you in your search for the herbs you want in your garden. This "creeping" rosemary grows low and about two feet wide and is one of the easiest herbs to grow in our area because of its ability to prosper in our sandy and sometimes poor soil. Unlike us, it does not mind the heat of our summers.

Be sure not to over water your rosemary and it too will become one of your favorite herbs. Rosemary has some Biblical associations with the Virgin Mary and in Egypt, boughs of rosemary was used

ROSMARINUS PROSTATES

CREEPING ROSEMARY

during some of the wedding ceremonies. It was also used as a disinfectant on the floors of early prisons and even in the judge's chambers and courts of justice. Greeks and Romans burned it as incense and old wives tales boast the ability of rosemary to ward off baldness. The next time you cook out on an open grill place a branch of rosemary in the flame to flavor your chicken, pork or fresh seafood!

Coming from an "Old Southern" family, I learned at an early age the devotion our mothers and Grandmothers had for the perennial herb Mint (*Mentha*). Not just for a tall glass of iced tea but also for another southern favorite a Mint Julep and more recently a Mojito. The fragrance of mint is easily recognizable and a small pinch of a leaf chewed will cleanse your breath. The variety that grows well and is popular for all our liquid refreshments is "Kentucky Colonel." This mint is extremely hearty and will sometimes take over your herb garden so remember to divide and conquer! A little afternoon shade will keep your patch of mint looking healthy during our hot summer afternoons and remember to harvest your mint early in the morning. Mint can be easily propagated by dividing and from stem cuttings.

In ancient Greek folklore the Greeks believed the God of the Underworld, "Pluto," became enraptured by the nymph "Menthe." Pluto's wife, being a jealous God's wife, did what every jealous wife would love to be able to do; she turned her adversary "Menthe" into a plant to forever grow in the shadows!

In Biblical times, people paid their taxes with mint leaves and it was also used to cure gum disease, indigestion, skin ulcers and to stimulate appetite. The next time you reach for that delicious bowl of vanilla ice cream after dinner try rubbing the bowl with some fresh mint leaves...yummy.

Storing and preserving herbs can be done by several methods but I choose to freeze my tender herbs like dill, fennel, tarragon, basil, chives and parsley. Harvest early in the morning, rinse off all dirt and sand, tie your herbs in a bundle with string. Blanch the bundle in boiling water for about 45 seconds and remove the bundle and place in ice water to cool. Remove the leaves from the stems after they have dried on a paper towel and place in a labeled plastic bag for the freezer. To dry herbs, I remove the big leaves from their stems and lay them on a cookie sheet. Turn the oven on to 150 degrees and when it reaches that temperature turn the oven off, Put the herbs in for no more than five minutes. Once they are dry, strip off the leaves and stack them in an airtight jar with a lid. Don't crush your herbs until you a ready to use them and enjoy!

Biography: Joan M. Thorington

To write about oneself can be somewhat difficult, "tooting your own horn" so to speak so let's start 58 years ago. I was born Sharron Lee Leyh in Germany and at 3 1/2 I was adopted by Air Force parents who were stationed in London. At the age of 5 we moved back to the states, A name change, Joan McFall Thorington (Joni to my friends), a naturalization process to become a citizen and my first participation in a flower show followed, I still have that first place ribbon in my jewelry box. And with great delight at the age of 9 the Camellia Society of South Carolina named a pink camellia after me.

Several years and many competitive swim meets later at the age of 13 I fell, severely breaking my ankle. The swim meets and aspirations of the Olympics went out the window so I went back to my first love, plants! Assisting my grandmother with her prize winning Dahlias and my mother's constant search for as many plants she could find in shades of lavender. I was also given recognition on several occasions for "yard of the month" wherever we were stationed.

I graduated from a boarding school in North Carolina, attended classes at Aum and Huntingdon College in Montgomery, Alabama. I graduated with a degree in Fine Arts from Faulkner and finished my education at the University of South Alabama in Mobile. Recognized as a fine arts photographer I sold my limited edition black & white photographs across the southeast with permanent collections of my works in Louisianna, Mississippi, Alabama, Florida and Georgia.

Fast forwarding through my debutante and junior league years I have a son who is 35 and lives with his wife in Montgomery , Alabama and I have lived in Fairhope, Alabama for 30 years. My attraction and awe of "mother earth's flora" was implanted as a young child by my Mother and Grandmother and continues to this day. I am employed by Jim Preast at Preast's Petals & Pottery on Gayfer Ext. in Fairhope , Alabama. I adore my job and truly enjoy sharing my knowledge and affection of plants with friends and frequent customers.

MENTHE

St. Augustine grass (*Stenotaphrum secundatum*), a favorite in the Gulf Region— course texture and tolerant of semi-shade.

Turf Grasses

Grasses for the Southern Home Landscape

By Dr. David Bransby

Grasses form a remarkably diverse family of plants. Their uses range from grain and sugar production (corn, wheat, oats, rye and sugarcane are all grasses) to forage for livestock, soil stabilization, wildlife habitat, lawns, ornamentals, and more recently, production of renewable energy. Their morphology is also highly diverse, ranging from a tree-like structure, such as that of bamboo, which is a grass, through bunch grasses that are often suitable as ornamentals, to creeping, sod-forming species that are commonly used in lawns.

This chapter provides a brief general overview of how grasses can be used in lawns, and as ornamental plants. However, it must be recognized that each of these two topics is the subject of many text books, so this presentation is only a very general guide, and does not replace the enormous volume of detailed information available on these subjects from other sources, including landscaping professionals in state extension systems, and at turf farms and commercial nurseries.

How Grasses Grow

All plants generate the organic tissue they are comprised of from

Bermuda — fine texture.

St. Augustine grass (*Stenotaphrum secundatum*).

photosynthesis, a process that makes use of energy from the sun, carbon dioxide absorbed from the air, and water from the soil to produce carbohydrates. Other nutrients absorbed from the soil facilitate production of proteins. Photosynthesis takes place mainly in the leaves. It makes sense, therefore, that when we grow many plants for grain, fruit or flowers, we take great care of their leaves by protecting them from diseases and insect pests; if the leaves are damaged it amounts to the factory of the plant being damaged. The result is lower yields of grains, fruit or flowers.

In contrast, for some of the roles that grasses serve, such as for forage and turf, we repeatedly defoliate them which means periodically stripping them of their leaves or factory. Despite this apparently devastating treatment, we expect them to continue with growth and production, and they do. Try doing this to most traditional ornamental plants, row crops, and trees, and see what happens. The result will be disastrous. So how have grasses become

adapted to defoliation? The answer to this is probably that they have become accustomed to repeated defoliation by large herds of animals or wildfires for millions of years, to the point that many of them actually need to be defoliated to keep them healthy.

Most grasses are sun loving plants that fall into one of two categories: sod forming or creeping grasses that form a dense mat just above the ground, and bunch grasses, with a strong vertical growth habit. Sod grasses are most commonly used for lawns, while most ornamentals are bunch grasses. The sod grasses can tolerate relatively close and frequent defoliation (such as mowing or grazing) because they have creeping stems that grow laterally, either above (stolons) or below (rhizomes) the ground. These creeping stems are home to many dormant buds, and they are storage sites for reserve carbohydrates. So when defoliated at even just an inch or two above the soil, they are still able to regenerate effectively. Bunch grasses are more tolerant of periodic defoliation than most other plants, but not as resilient as sod grasses.

Lawns

Lawns are among the most visually pleasing features of any home landscape, but they also require a lot of attention, including mowing, fertilization, irrigation and weed control. The challenge is to accomplish effective lawn care without letting it get to you—convince yourself that resisting purchase of a riding lawnmower is good for your health, or if you buy one, you come up with your best ideas during the countless hours you spend alone riding on it— and even disposing of the pet droppings before you mow provides fertilizer for the flower garden and is fun!

Grass Species

Typically, one inherits whatever grass is in the lawn when you buy a home, unless you purchase

Zoysia grass — fine texture.

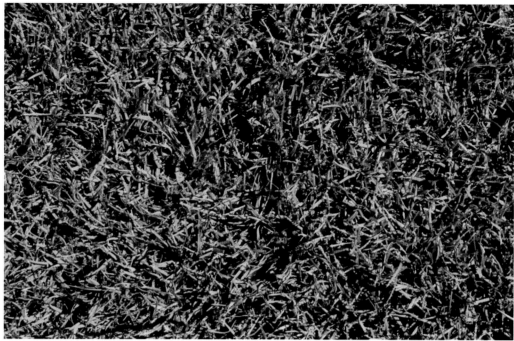

Seashore paspalum (*Paspalum vaginatum*)

a new home prior to initiation of any landscaping activity. Therefore, unless one chooses to replace an existing lawn, the opportunity to select a lawn grass is relatively rare. Having said that, even if you inherit a lawn when you buy a home, or if you have a yard service take care of your lawn, it is useful to know at least a little about different lawn grasses and how they should be maintained.

It should also be recognized that the only way to make sure about the species of any plant one is interested in is to check on its scientific or botanical name, rather than a common name. The reason for this is that different plants are often referred to by means of the same common name, and the same plant can have several common names. This can clearly cause confusion, so the botanical names of all plants referenced in this chapter are provided at least once. It is also important to understand that there are usually several genetically improved varieties of most plant species that that have been in commercial use for any length of time: plant geneticists typically improve plants for resistance to factors such as pests, diseases and drought. This work is ongoing, which means that new, improved varieties continue to enter the market. The obvious implication of this genetic improvement is that to get the best available grass for whatever your purpose, it is best to survey not only different species, but also different varieties within species.

Lawn grasses vary in texture. Those that have relatively broad leaves, such as St. Augustine centipede, carpet and bahiagrass, are known as course textured, while those that have intermediate leaf width such as seashore paspalum are medium textured, and species like bermudagrass and zoysia grass are fine textured. Grasses also vary with respect to shade, with St. Augustine and zoysia being more tolerant than the others. However, most lawn grasses are inherently sun loving plants, and none will do well in more than about fifty percent shade. So if you have spots in the landscape that are in heavy shade, do not subject yourself to the frustration of trying to successfully establish a lawn in these locations. Develop an alternative strategy by simply covering the area with pine needle or bark mulch, and/or establishing a flower bed of shade–tolerant ornamentals.

While perfectly manicured lawns containing a single grass species may be appealing to the eye, lawns that contain a mixture of grasses are often just as appealing if mown regularly, even if they contain species like bahiagrass. In fact, a large proportion of lawns

Annual ryegrass (*Lolium multiflorum*), commonly used to oversow perennial lawns to provide bright green color in winter, but also to possibly attract wildlife away from damaging valuable ornamental plants.

Seashore paspalum (*Paspalum vaginatum*) growing here, within feet of salt water in Mobile Bay —medium texture and obviously tolerant of saline soils.

On the other hand, you may not want to give up that wonderful exercise or all those ideas you get while you are mowing. An attractive green lawn in winter can be achieved by oversowing your summer lawn with annual ryegrass. Besides the visual benefits provided by this winter lawn, ryegrass is a favorite feed among several wildlife species. Therefore, on the one hand, it is likely to attract these animals, and on the other, it might well distract them from damaging valuable ornamentals or vegetables at a time of the year where their preferred feed is scarce in certain locales.

Mowing

While most of us consider mowing to be a chore, it is really not hard to convince yourself that it is fun. After all, positive visual results after mowing are really rewarding, especially when compared to other chores like washing dishes and cleaning house. Mowing requires several key considerations, especially cutting height, cutting frequency, and mulching versus bagging.

Always remember that when you mow you are removing the factory (leaves) of the plant on the one hand, and on the other, grasses need to be defoliated in order to remain healthy. This means that there is an optimum mowing regime for lawns, located between mowing too frequently and too short, and too infrequently and too tall. This optimum varies among different grasses: for St Augustine grass, optimal cutting height is about 3 inches, or around the highest setting on most mowers, while for bermuda- and bahiagrass it is 1 to 2 inches, with seashore paspalum intermediate. Mowing frequency is determined primarily by growth rate: the faster the growth, the more frequently the lawn should be mowed. Mowing too often and too short can weaken the lawn and cause spots to die. Cutting too infrequently often leaves the lawn looking pale green after mowing, or even brown in some cases, and can allow the accumulation of too much thatch which can restrict water and fertilizer from reaching the soil where it is needed.

Development of mulching lawnmowers has been a boon to homeowners by reducing time involved with bagging, as well as fertilizer needs. These mowers cut and chop the grass, and force the cut particles into the canopy of the lawn where they decay and return nutrients and organic matter to the soil with little or no negative visual effect. In contrast, bagging and removing cut grass from the lawn involves more work and amounts to removal of nutrients from the area, thus increasing the fertilizer requirement.

Maintenance

In addition to being mown, lawns may need to be fertilized, irrigated and treated for weeds, diseases and pests. In the interest of the environment, these activities should be kept to a minimum: water is becoming more and more scarce, and use of strong chemicals in fertilizers, pesticides and insecticides can be harmful, especially if

surrounding older homes fall into this category, and there is a distinct trend for species diversity in any landscape to be "environmentally cool." So consider living with what you have, instead of replacing it. This also makes ecological sense, especially in lawns that cover a large heterogeneous area: even though a single species of grass might have been planted when the lawn was established, other grasses migrate in over time and establish in spots where they are better adapted to local soil or shade conditions.

Most lawn grasses used in the Gulf Region are warm season perennials. This means that they go dormant in winter, and top growth actually dies and browns off if frost occurs. You might be happy to accept this appearance, and enjoy the break from mowing.

Bahiagrass seedheads can emerge within 24 to 48 hours after mowing, something you may not want.

applied in excessive amounts.

While lime is not really a fertilizer, its application to lawns is critically important because it is used to adjust the acidity or pH of the soil. Soils in the Gulf Region are typically acid (pH less than 6.0, and sometimes below 5.0). While most woody plants such as trees, shrubs like azaleas, and other ornamentals do fine in acid soils, in general, grasses grow better when soils are less acid (pH = 6.0 or higher). The only way to tell whether lime is needed is to take a soil sample and have it tested. Such tests are conducted at labs run by land grant universities. They can usually be arranged through your local county extension office, and will normally cost no more than $10.00. The way you collect these samples is particularly important. The aim is to get a representative average for your entire lawn. This means that it is best to take ten to twenty small samples from across your entire lawn. Ideally, these should be obtained with a soil auger, but a narrow trowel will also work. These samples are then combined and mixed thoroughly in a bucket. Once this has been done, the soil in the bucket can be sub-sampled for lab analysis which will provide information that will include the amount of lime, phosphorous and potassium that is needed.

Nitrogen is the most important nutrient for lawns, but because it is very mobile compared to phosphorous and potassium, its level in the soil can fluctuate substantially over time. This makes estimates of nitrogen in soil samples of relatively little value, so nitrogen fertilizer is typically applied according to an estimate of plant needs which are usually described on the fertilizer bag. Recommended application rates are usually expressed in pounds per unit area (thousand square feet). In this regard, it must be emphasized that accurate application rates are very important, because over application of nitrogen fertilizer can seriously contaminate ground and surface water. In addition, application of nitrogen fertilizer may cause an increase in soil acidity, thus requiring repeated application of lime. In view of this, soil tests should ideally be conducted every 3 to 5 years, and lawns should be fertilized sparingly, no more often than once a year, but in some cases, as infrequently as once every 2 to 4 years. Finally, lawns should be fertilized at the beginning of the growing season when growth conditions are good, and never during droughts unless prior to irrigation, because this can seriously damage the lawn.

With the steady expansion of the population and periodic droughts, clean water is becoming an increasingly precious commodity. Irrigation should therefore be applied to lawns sparingly, and only to prevent them from dying. In this regard, many lawn grasses are surprisingly tough, and simply go dormant in a drought, recovering remarkably well as soon as the drought breaks. Control of diseases and pests in lawns is often complex and challenging. Therefore, if problems of this kind are suspected it is probably advisable to get the help of lawn professionals.

This page and opposite: Two different types of Pampasgrass. The Point? There can be substantial differences among different varieties of the same species, and this must berecognized when making choices.

Ornamental Grasses

Ornamentals

By Dr. David Bransby

Twenty years ago very few grasses were used as ornamentals, perhaps because grasses mostly had a weed image in relation to plants that were typically planted in flower beds. That has changed dramatically, and there are now literally dozens of ornamental grasses available from ornamental nurseries. Advantages using grasses as ornamentals include the following:

1. Adapted to low fertility
2. Often reach their peak in fall
3. Combine well with many flowering plants
4. Attractive in planters
5. Excellent for dry flower arrangements
6. Tolerant of drought
7. Largely resistant to pests and diseases
8. Require very little maintenance
9. Provide habitat for birds and wildlife
10. Adapted to a wide range of soil conditions
11. Improve soil with extensive roots
12. Stabilize soil on slopes

In contrast to lawn grasses, for which opportunities to purchase new material are limited, you can always add ornamental grasses to the landscape. In this regard, as for lawn grasses, genetic variation among varieties of the same species can be substantial. For example, all varieties of Pampas grass are not equal. Some have plumes held well above the leaves, and others have plumes almost embedded in the leaves. In addition, some have cream plumes, while others have pinkish plumes. In view of this it is advisable to make sure that there are photographs of mature plants attached to juvenile plants at nurseries to facilitate informed selection. One word of warning: several ornamental grasses are classified as serious invasive species, and these should be avoided.

Above: Grasses combine well with flowers in planters.

Above and below: Switchgrass (*Panicum virgatum*), a well known native plant being developed for production of renewable energy, can be used for landscaping and is a popular nesting location for redwing black birds.

As mentioned earlier, ornamental grasses require little maintenance, including no fertilizer or irrigation. In fact, fertilization can often make them too tall, thus causing them to fall over. To facilitate healthy growth in spring, most ornamental grasses should be pruned back to a height of 12 to 24 inches. Be sure to not cut them too short, because bunch grasses are sensitive to close defoliation. Also, do not burn them because this is dangerous – the residual material actually makes a great mulch, especially if run through a shredder.

Have fun getting hooked on grass!

Biography: Dr. David Bransby

Dr. David Bransby is a Professor of Energy Crops and Bioenergy in the Department of Agronomy and Soils at Auburn University. He was raised on a small dairy farm in South Africa, and holds BS and PhD degrees in Grassland Science from the University of Natal in that country, and a MS in Agronomy from the University of Missouri – Columbia. He immigrated from South Africa in 1987, and is a naturalized US citizen. Dr. Bransby has over 30 years of experience in agronomic research, and has spent 20 years specializing in the production and processing of energy crops, a subject in which he has an international reputation. He has 321 technical publications, serves on the editorial boards of two international bioenergy journals, and consults for several private bioenergy companies. In September of 2006 Dr. Bransby was asked to brief Governor Riley of Alabama and President Bush on the status of the emerging biofuels industry. In February 2007 he was invited to the White House to advise President Bush, Secretary of Energy Sam Bodman and senior White House officials on the feasibility of large scale cellulosic biofuel production in the United States over the next 10 years.

ONE YOU NO NOT WANT! Opposite: Cogon grass (*Imperata cylindrica*)—to the uninformed this plant may appear to be an attractive candidate for use as an ornamental, but it is one of the most serious invasive species in the Gulf region. The tiny, fluffy seeds travel for miles on even a light breeze. It establishes quickly and spreads aggressively even in the presence of competition, and is dominating many highway right of ways. Cogon grass is costly to eradicate, and poses a fire hazard in winter.

At right: Fountain grass (*Pennisetum setaceum*) and petunias.

Small patches of oats (*Avena sativa*; above) and Barley (*Hordeum vulgare*; below) are attractive in the landscape, and useful for dry arrangements in spring and summer.

Dwarf miscanthus (*Miscanthus sinensus*) mixes well with a wide variety of other ornamental plants.

Shrubs

These Wonderful Woody Plants, With Two or More
Stems Arising From Their Bases, Vary in Size, Shape
and Coloration to Provide Structure and to Serve as
a Foundation for Our Yards and Gardens.

By Rosemary Hart, Bea Sheldon and Lois Boykin

Their rapid growth and maturity, as compared to trees, enable
us to establish highly attractive yards and gardens in a relatively
short time.

The variability of shrub usage can create outstanding designs
on a small lot or a large estate. A single shrub can serve as an
accent plant or as a natural garden sculpture. A mass of shrubs
can decorate, define boundaries, provide shade or windbreaks,
or cover a garage or unsightly area.

Shrubs vary greatly in size and shape. Some are used as ground
covers, and lesser or dwarf shrubs may be only two or three feet
high. Taller shrubs may reach heights of twenty feet. Shapes may be
upright, spreading, rounded, arching, or even tree shaped.

The coastal climate of Baldwin and Mobile County is conducive
to shrub growth. Early spring and fall temperatures give us two
good seasons to plant shrubs. Winter and summer months require
greater attention to mulching and watering. Continual and rapid
growth of some shrubs should cause us to give careful consideration
to plant and site selection as well as soil preparation and planting
procedure.

Plant selection naturally involves foliage and flowers, but primary consideration should be given to growth habits, hardiness, and insect and disease resistance. Native shrubs are adapted to our climate and soils, and they are usually highly successful if planted appropriately.

Equally as important as plant selection is site selection. The site location should match the plant's needs with regard to wet or dry soil, sun or shade, and the ultimate size in terms of both height and width of the shrub.

Soil condition and planting procedures used with shrubs are critical to plant success. It is important to test for soil conditions and to provide amendments as needed. Soil test kits are available from plant and nursery dealers and Cooperative Extension System offices in both coastal counties. Good planting practices will help establish the shrub and provide for healthy development. We recommend the following:

↗ The area to be planted should be dug at least a foot deeper and two to three times as wide as the root ball of the shrub.

↗ Amendments, as required, should be mixed with the loosened soil from the hole.

↗ Gently loosen the outside and bottom roots, spreading them outward to encourage growth.

↗ Place the shrub so that the top of the container soil is slightly higher than ground level on each side of the hole, remembering that the plant may settle as water is added to the hole.

↗ Add soil taken from the hole and a little water as needed to eliminate air pockets.

↗ With planting completed, water the shrub slowly but well, and mulch a few inches away from the stem and outward to help the shrub maintain moisture.

↗ Weekly slow, deep watering for the first few seasons should firmly establish the plant.

Once established, foliage, blooms, and fruit or berries can provide year-round points of interest in our yards. Our selections of sixteen of the hardiest deciduous and evergreen shrubs seen in Baldwin and Mobile County are described below.

Bananashrub
Michelia figo or Michelia skinneriana

This dense shrub can be located by its banana-scented flowers in early spring. It has small, shiny, dark evergreen leaves and grows to a height of fifteen feet. It likes well-drained soil and sun or partial shade. Pruning is not required, but can be done to promote flowering and to create a tree form. Bananashrub requires little care and seems to be disease and insect resistant.

Bottlebrush
Callistemon citrinus

The common name describes this erect, five to ten foot erect shrub. The spreading branches have long narrow leaves with "brush-like" flower spikes at stem ends. The summer flowers have red stamens longer than the flower petals, and are attractive to birds. Bottlebrush grows well in average soil, liking sun or partial shade. It is said to be salt tolerant.

Boxwood
Buxus sempervirens

To create structure, a cottage or more formal garden appearance, use English boxwood. The finger-

nail size, deep green leaves are attractive year-round. Plants can be pruned to create square, round, or artistically shaped forms. Pruning is best done in late winter to early fall and promotes dense growth. Maintain a broad base and somewhat narrow top when pruning. This helps prevent shading of lower branches which can cause leaf loss and a "leggy" look. Boxwood varieties range in height from two to twenty feet. (Box has many problems in our climate. Sometimes it fares satisfactorily, but often it does not thrive. Yaupon cultivars, like "Bordeaux," which look like Box do much better here.)

Bridlewreath
Spirea prunifolia

A walkway cascading with bridlewreath is a pathway suitable for a spring or summer bride. This spirea has masses of arching stems lined with delicate, narrow leaves and clusters of small single or double yellow or white flowers. It thrives in moist, well-drained soil, growing to a height of about eight feet. Partial shade will keep the leaves from scorching. Pruning after flowering is helpful, but this shrub fares well even with neglect.

Cleyera
Ternstroemia gymnanthera

For glossy, evergreen foliage, cleyera is a southern gardener's choice. Thumb-sized leaves are dark green on top and seem to swirl about the end of reddish stems. New leaves are copper-colored, and are often seen if the plant is pruned frequently. Creamy white, fragrant flowers appear in spring, and dull red berries are produced in the fall. This shrub can be pruned often and kept under three feet, or allowed to grow to fifteen feet. It grows quickly as a border or screen, and can be pruned to tree form as a specimen plant. It likes well-drained soil and tolerates full sun or partial shade. Be sure to plant it in a wide hole to enhance growth.

Crapemyrtle
Lagerstroemia indica

Described as either a tree or shrub, this deciduous summer-flowering plant is common along roadways and in our yards. Pruned to tree form, the trunks, in light brown or taupe with dark splotches, are singularly spectacular. The medium green, oval shaped leaves turn to stunning yellow, orange or red in the fall. If these trunks and fall leaves do not capture your attention, the crinkled flower petals blooming from mid-June through September will. The small "crepe paper" flower petals mass along the outer edges of stems into panicles six to eight inches long and three to five inches wide. The popsicle colors range from white, light, medium, or dark pink to lavender and red. The flower scent is light and lovely. The plant grows best in moist well-drained soil in full sun. Cultivar selections range from shrublike forms from three to five feet or tree size forms up to thirty-five feet. They can be propagated from seeds or cuttings, and they are easily transplanted in fall or late winter. Crapemyrtles are often unnecessarily severely pruned. Late winter is

the time to thin unwanted trunks at ground level or cluttered limbs at their point of origin. Light pruning of pencil thin growth in midsummer can also be done but heavy pruning is generally not recommended.

Hollies
Ilex spp.

There are hundreds of evergreen and deciduous holly species, hybrids, and cultivars, and more than a dozen of the most desirable

themselves to containers, small, mounded shapes of about three feet, or hedge shapes to eight feet. They are shallow –rooted, and tend to fall over if pruned into tall tree forms. Serrated leaves are dark green and shiny. The plant has mildly, fragrant white or pink flowers in the spring and black berries in the fall. Foliage, flowers and fruit make Indian Hawthorne attractive year-round. It likes moist, well-drained soil and sun or part shade. It is salt-tolerant, but somewhat susceptible to leaf spot and fire blight. An organic mulch of wood chips or shredded bark will help to keep disease spores from splashing up on the plant. Winter pruning of diseased leaves will also help to reduce the chances of infections.

Leatherleaf Mahonia
Mahonia bealei

A striking plant, Leatherleaf Mahonia is upright, with three to six or more stems originating in a central clump or crown. Stems are topped with coarse, spiny, leather-like blue-green leaves about three inches long. Clusters of pale yellow flowers flow from stem tops in late winter or early spring. The flowers are followed by light bluish berries which hang like grapes along the ends of the stems. This plant likes moist but   well-drained soil. It grows four to ten feet tall, but can be pruned by cutting old or leggy stems back to the top of the clump. New stems will sprout and the clump can be divided if more than one of these specimen plants is desired. This shrub likes shady garden spots, and the birds love the berries.

Loropetalum
Loropetalum chinense

This evergreen shrub with green or burgundy foliage can be allowed to grow naturally to a wide, rounded shape, or it can be heavily pruned. The small oval leaves create a great background for the white, pink, or burgundy spring flowers. Small clusters of flowers along the stems are light and feathery in appearance. "Purple Pixie" is a low-growing cultivar about three feet high and wide. Generally, however, this shrub is six to twelve feet high unless pruned regularly. It likes moist, well-drained soil and full sun or partial shade.

Oleander
Nerium oleander

A lazy summer drive or a day at the beach will enable you to see numerous and glorious oleander blooms. This broad, rounded, fine textured, six to twelve foot shrub has narrow gray-green leaves and single or double flower clusters in white, pink, rose, or pale yellow. It grows in any well-drained soil in full sun. If planted in shade it is prone to mildew, and scales can turn the leaves yellow. Fortunately, badly infested branches can be pruned out, and scale can usually be eliminated by spraying with dormant oil in late winter. It is said that all plant parts are poisonous if eaten, and burning the wood can be irritating to eyes and skin. Generally, oleander requires no care except occasional pruning of old wood in spring or light pruning to promote plant growth. This fast-growing plant looks great in pots, or as a free form hedge or border.

Pittosporum
Pittosporum tobira

Landscapers must love this evergreen shrub. The glossy, medi-

are native to South Alabama. Grown for their bright green foliage and glossy red berries, they make great container plants, border and hedging plants, and privacy screens. Hollies like well-drained soil and sun or partial shade. Problems may occur if they are planted under the dripline of house eaves, or if the plants are planted too close together. Hollies can be pruned heavily in winter or early spring, or tip-pruned to encourage dense foliage. The eventual sizes of hollies should be carefully considered when selecting planting sites. Most range in height from three feet to fifteen feet, but a few, such as American Holly, Ilex Americana, and Dahoon Holly, Ilex cassine, will eventually grow into medium-sized trees. The hollies in general do not like to be transplanted.

Indian Hawthorne
Raphiolepsis indica

This evergreen shrub is available in numerous varieties, lending

um textured dark green foliage is rounded and spreading. It grows rapidly to 12 feet tall in well-drained soil, in full sun or partial shade. Pittosporum can be pruned as a hedge or topiary. It has clusters of white and dull yellow, fragrant flowers in spring and occasional ornamental fruits in fall. Variegated forms are popular as are some dwarf varieties. This is a low maintenance plant, but can be fertilized in early spring with 12-6-6 tree and shrub fertilizer. After first frost, a light application of 5-10-10 low-nitrogen fertilizer will keep it healthy until spring. Pittosporum is vulnerable to scale but can be treated with horticultural oil.

Sweet Olive
Osmanthus fragrans

An old-fashioned evergreen shrub, Sweet Olive will perfume your yard and your neighbor's yard in the fall and winter. The thick leaves have a dark green luster with spiny edges. Tiny white, jasmine-scented flowers sprout along the stems. The plant grows slowly in an irregular, upright form, to a height of ten to fifteen feet. It grows in moist, well-drained soil in sun or partial shade. Pruning is usually limited to late winter for the removal of dead wood.

Wax Myrtle
Myrica cerifera

This is a large evergreen native shrub with aromatic, olive colored, pointed leaves, white spring flowers and waxy gray-green berries clustered along twigs. This plant likes moist, well-drained soil in sun or light shade. It does not require pruning except to remove deadwood in winter. The clippings are said to be a flea-repellant for dog beds. In colonial times, wax from the berries was used to make candles. It eventually grows to twenty feet tall, and if not pruned to hedge or tree form, it can grow almost as wide as it is tall. Wax Myrtle is a large, durable, trouble-free shrub for barriers and informal hedges.

Gardenia
Gardenia jasminoides

One cannot describe life in the gentle South without mentioning the Gardenia. This elegant lady is found guarding the border of the yard; providing a back ground for bright perennials; in large groupings on the side yard with azaleas and bridal wreath and; in (small varieties) in containers on decks and patios. Where ever this lady stands, she shares her sweet fragrances all around to the delight of the family! As much as wide porches with swings and rocking chairs, memories of lemonade in tall pitchers, this dark green bush with its white velvet flowers reminds us of home.

A very hardy plant, Gardenias may be rooted from tiny cuttings during blooming. Gardenia flourish in full sun or light shade but require an acid soil that drains well. Old leaves are shed as temperatures heat. Gardenias do, however, suffer from white flies whose sugary excrement drops on the leaves and a black sooty mod will grow. This is easily washed off the leaves with soapy water.

All in all, Gardenias are very easily grown in our area—enjoy!

To root: When you cut your blooms for your home, leave the stems in water until roots form. Then plant in soil in a protected area until cold weather when they may be transplanted to your garden.

Hydrangea
Hydrangea sp

No Southern yard is complete without a Hydrangea or two. This deciduous shrub makes a great background plant or the vocal point in your garden. Most Hydrangeas like light shade for our hot summers. They especially like to be shaded from the afternoon sun. However, new varieties have been developed that take full sun.

Hydrangeas have large leaves with showy clusters of long-lasting blooms that range in colors from white, pink, red, lavender to blue depending on the soil. Acid soil (side dress with aluminum sulphate) produce blue and lavender flowers while alkaline soil (side dress with lime) produce reds and pinks. Neutral soil will often produce white. Hydrangeas have woody stems and dark green oval leaves with serrated edges. These wonderful shrubs are tough plants that thrive in moist, humus-rich, but well drained soil and can grow to be ten feet tall and eight feet wide. Most hydrangeas bloom on previous year's growth so prune in the late winter to remove old or dead wood, spent blooms or over growth. A great way to prune is to cut these wonderful flowers to enjoy in your home. Many varieties will dry as the water evaporates and you can enjoy them in dried arrangements. The best time to pick the blooms is in the early morning.

Hydrangea cuttings can be rooted from softwood in the summer or hardwood in the winter.

Oak leaf Hydrangea
Hydrangea quercefolia

The Oak leaf Hydrangea is native to Alabama and grows wild in our forest and woods. Many shady yards are landscaped with this variety. These plants can grow to be over six feet tall with large oak shaped leaves that turn bronze to crimson in the fall. The blooms come in the late spring to early summer and are long and white that will turn light purple as they age. This variety is also deciduous and needs to be pruned in the winter. Cuttings can be rooted to add new plants to your garden.

Many brides are using the hydrangeas blooms in wedding bouquets and arrangements as they last so well and are so striking in appearance.

Roses

Roses Have Always Been the Epitome of Fine Gardening But Have Often Carried the Reputation of Being Difficult to Grow.

By Linda Guy

While it is true that most roses require extra attention, for the hobbyist who enjoys working in their yard, roses are very attainable, even in the deep South. This is seen in many of the fine rose gardens across the upper gulf coast both public and private.

There are several key basics that should be learned and practiced if success with roses is to be achieved. The first is location. Roses love sunshine and languish in the shade. The spot chosen for a

rose bed should receive at least six to eight hours of direct sun each day. Also, roses love water but require good drainage so be sure the area you chose is well drained. Once this is determined, building the bed is the next step. While it is tempting to take short cuts in this area, investing the time proper soil preparation will pay big dividends in the long run. The roses bushes you will plant will only be as good as their root system will support, so planning for great roots will produce great bushes.

The soil should be worked a minimum of 18 inches deep by adding organic material and soil conditioners. This can be purchased materials such as peat moss, bark, perlite, and vermiculite or it can be the homemade variety made from collected materials such as leaves, manures, kitchen waste, etc. If your location is one of the many areas

that has a heavy clay substructure, you might consider raised beds to resolve drainage problems that are common to heavy clay. Sandy soils on the other hand rarely have drainage problems but because they are so porous, nutrients are difficult to retain. The key to correcting both types of soil, however, is the same—add organic content.

The best time to plan and build rose beds is in the fall when there is plenty of time and materials available for this chore. If done at this time organic material can be worked in the bed to compost "in place" ready for spring planting. This would also be a good time to determine irrigation preferences since "in ground" systems should be installed prior to planting.

When you are ready to plant, choosing the right varieties is criti-

cal. Roses, like people, have climatic preferences. Choosing varieties that don't like the hot humid gulf coast weather will be disastrous, or at least disappointing for even the most dedicated rosarian. Visiting other gardens to see what varieties flourish in our climate is good way to decide what you like. Making a list to take when you shop is an excellent way to keep your focus on heat tolerant varieties. Chose well potted and maintained, grade 1 plants from reputable nurseries. The leaves and canes should be clear of spots that might indicate disease problems. Never purchase wax coated bushes that are usually available at "bargain" prices since these rarely survive in the long run. (A list of recommended varieties is included) If you must order the varieties you chose, they will most likely be delivered bare

root. Bare root roses should be soaked in water for 12-24 hours before planting. While planting these roses directly into the ground will work, potting and growing them off for 8-10 weeks in a 3- gallon pot will achieve much better results in terms of faster root development.

Fertilizing roses once they are planted is essential for good roses. Roses are heavy feeders and require a steady diet to thrive. Best results are achieved by having a soil test done and learning what nutrients are available or missing from the soil. Generally, however,

the coastal areas require a steady replacement of nitrogen which is often leached out by rainfall and irrigation, very little phosphorous as it occurs naturally in most of our soils, and some potassium. Sources for these major nutrients can be either synthethic such as those you purchase in the local garden center, or organic such alfalfa, cotton seed meal, etc. Organic sources are especially recommended on newly planted bushes that have tender roots that are easily burned. Local feed stores are excellent resources for these fertilizers. Don't neglect to monitor the pH of your soil when fertilizing since

soil that is too acid will result in poor uptake of nutrients and virtual starvation for your roses. The acid that is common on the coast is easily remedied with routine applications of dolomitic lime that can be found at all gardens centers.

Water is the life blood of all plants and roses are no exception. Roses generally require about 2 inches of water per week but during hot dry periods more may necessary. A reliable irrigation system will keep watering chores at a minimum.

Removing spent blooms or even cutting prime blooms for home decoration will keep roses producing on a regular basis.

Alas, every garden has it's serpent and for the rosarian it's name is "Black Spot." Fungus control in roses is the one chore that gives rose growing its bad reputation. To have beautiful healthy roses one must commit to a regular spray schedule to control fungus. Research in recent years has reduced the

Rose illustration by Louise Estes

frequency but not the need to spray. Consulting rosarians with American Rose Society can give you a handle on the current most effective controls as chemicals often come and go. Once you have selected your fungicides, ALWAYS follow label directions for application rates and personal protection. Don't let the word "chemical" scare you away since there are fungicides available that are as safe or safer to use than many household cleaners. Meanwhile, testing is ongoing to produce more resistant varieties of roses so that the need to spray will be further reduced.

Further information on growing roses is always available by contacting the American Rose Society in Shreveport, LA (www.ars.org) which can put you in touch with local societies and rosarians for continuing education on growing the "Queen of Flowers."

Biography: Linda Guy

I have been the rose horticulturist at Bellingrath Gardens since 1984. I also specialize in butterfly gardening at Bellingrath and have been in charge of the conservatory for the last 12 years. I am married to John Guy, who is also a horticulturist in charge of lawns and irrigation at Bellingrath. I have a masters degree in Religious Education which I employ on a voluntary basis in the children's ministry at Cottage Hill Baptist Church in Mobile.

Louise Estes

Camellia japonica "Bella Romano," antique variety with a classical European look.

Camellias

Camellia japonica "Asian Artistry," a recent Green Nurseries introduction pays homage to the simpler form of camellias greatly admired in Japan.

The Blossom of Winter

Text and photos by Bobby Green

The camellia was introduced into western civilization around 300 years ago when plants of *Camellia japonica* were mistakenly substituted for *Camellia sinensis* (tea plants) in an order bound for Great Britain. The boldly flowering "tree of shining leaves" created a widespread sensation, quickly becoming the rage in European gardens, art and fashion.

Arriving in America just over 200 years ago, the camellia quickly became a naturalized citizen, settling primarily in the coastal areas of the Deep South. Here, a friendly climate and the hospitality of excit-

ed gardeners welcomed the discovery like a lost child returning to its rightful home. The wondrously flowering evergreen became an anchor of Southern gardens proudly representing the grace and charm associated with the Old South.

Camellias went in and out of fashion until the mid-1940s, when ever-unpredictable public interest spurred a resurrection in popularity. Gardeners and collectors formed clubs of local, state and national scope to share information and growing fascination with camellias. Camellia shows became as popular as camellia balls. Bestselling novelist Frances Parkinson Keyes was particularly fascinated by the blossom, sprinkling her New Orleans-based tales with descriptions of its beauty, and even went so far as to base an entire book about the development of a blue variety. (Unfortunately, the blue camellia lives on only within the realm of fiction.) Alabama heralded the spectacular, adopted bloom as its state flower—probably to the envy of its attractive, but more humble native blossoms.

The renewed excitement of the forties and fifties created greater demands for camellia growers to develop new and different flowers. Hybridizers fed hungry appetites with dozens of introductions each year. New species of camellia were discovered and crossed with familiar japonicas to produce blooms of expanded size, different color, or sweet fragrance.

Today there are more than 20,000 registered camellias with more introductions debuting each year. Camellia nurseries continue to search for the elusive new bloom that will forever transfix the demanding devotee.

Above: *Camellia japonica* "Ohkan," a "Higo" camellia-style favored by the Samurai. Opposite page: Camella hybrid "Delores Edwards," one of the best all-around garden camellias.

semi-double flowers are violet-red mottled in white, and are particularly striking when the variegation is patterned with a blotch of white on each of the long slender petals. Blooms are seen all season, on a compact, rounded plant. The original dates to 1954. We believe this is another overlooked variety that is truly different.

Sea Foam. This shrub has seen a revival of interest, due to its excellent flowers. The large formal double is a white and many-petaled. Sea Foam blooms late in the season in a strong, upright plant. Released by J. T. Weisner in Florida in 1959.

A Sampler of Some Favorite Camellias

We are fortunate to be in a location where camellias have been highly prized. The area around Mobile and Baldwin County has been a camellia Mecca for nearly a century, echoing with the names of Sawada, Rubel, Haynie and other camellia pioneers who explored that particularly glorious floral world and expanded its horizons. We have roamed Mobile and outlying areas, looking for camellia treasures left by these pioneers. We have discovered old gardens and nursery sites where these legendary men worked. We have uncovered ancient camellias in cemeteries, dilapidated home sites, and private collections.

While these half-century-old plants may seem old by some standards, in camellia chronology they are relatively young. Camellias hundreds of years old have been discovered at remote temples in Japan, where it was believed that the gods lived in their blooms on visits to the earthly realm.

Heirloom (1950-1959)

Edna Campbell Variegated. We were first intrigued by this most unique flower when we stumped upon an abandoned garden. The

Modern (1960-)

Dahlohnega. This camellia has attracted much interest since its 1986 introduction, and deservedly so. The small-to-medium flowers are formal double—a most beautiful antique white with light yellow shading. We are very impressed both with the flower and the good growth habit—compact, upright and rather slow, but vigorous. Despite its relatively "newborn" status, Dahlohnega can stand beside the all-time great camellias.

Sawada's Mahogany. We have yet to find the person who can identify this most unique flower. The original was found in the Mobile garden of renowned camellian K. Sawada. Apparently the flowers had been the talk of the neighborhood for years. The plant is quite vigorous and produces large anemone-to-peony-form flowers early in the season. The color is best described as a mahogany-red with a violet tint. We have never seen it's duplicate and are half-convinced it is another of the late Mr. Sawada's extraordinary seedlings.

Tama No Ura. If the flower of the beautiful Tama No Ura was borne on the most spindly of shrubs, it would still be widely grown. Indescribably charming flowers are simple, single, red-bordered white, reminding one of peppermint candy. This variety blooms profusely on a graceful, somewhat pendulous, shrub. Imported from Japan to the U. S. in 1973, it is one of the favorites in our garden.

Garden Hybrid Camellias

Delores Edwards. (1989) *C. x williamsii* Large, light orchid-pink flowers adorn this vigorous grower during mid-season. The flowers are a beautiful semi-double to anemone to peony, but the good growth habits attracted our attention as well. From Hulyn Smith of Valdosta, GA

Tiny Princess. (1961) *C. fraternal x 'Akebono'* Originated by K. Sawada, this unique camellia can still be found in old gardens of our area, although it is mostly unknown today. When people see it bloom, they instantly fall in love with its miniature semi-double to loose peony-form delicate pink-and-white flowers,

which appear in great profusion during midseason. The slow, spreading, open growth is distinctly bronze. Tiny Princess will eventually make a large shrub, perfect for the border or against a fence wall. This is another fragrant camellia.

Camellia Sasanquas

Leslie Ann. (*C. sasanqua*, 1958) Fast becoming one of the most popular of the fall blooming camellias, this creation of the Ray Davis Nursery blooms so heavily it nearly hides the foliage. The charming white flowers have a picoteed magenta edging. Upright and compact habit.

Rose of Autumn. (*C hiemalis*, 1990) Of the hundreds of our own sasanqua seedlings to have bloomed in the past 15 years at the nursery this is by far the best. Large, many-petaled semi-double flowers are a warm rose color with a wavy edge. A sheen upon the bloom seems to give a glow to the flowers at dusk. Vigorous, upright growth with dark green leaves.

Stephanie Golden. (*C sasanqua*, 1980s) This magnificent shrub should one day win the coveted Ralph Peer Award, the highest honor bestowed upon a C. sasanqua and its relatives. Very compact, upright and dense growth. Flowers are a strong clear pink in great profusion over a long period. Exceptional selection from Tom Dodd Jr., of Semmes, Alabama.

Camellia Culture

Planting. Good drainage is vital for healthy camellias. To ensure proper drainage, plant camellias slightly above ground, with the top of the root ball one to two inches above grade. The hole should be twice the diameter of the root ball. Be sure to remove plastic shipping bag from new plants. After setting the new plant in the hole, fill with a prepared soil mixture, water thoroughly and tamp, making sure that the elevated portion of the root ball is lightly covered. Mulch freely with pine straw, bark, or other organic matter.

Soil. Camellias generally thrive in a well-drained, slightly acidic soil high in humus. A choice planting mixture would be an equal portion of soil (preferably sandy loam) and a porous, prepared planting mix.

Watering. Camellias, especially newly-planted ones, need moisture to remain healthy.

This does not mean that the root system should stay wet. In humid climates such as the Gulf Coast region, two or three (depending upon sun exposure and dryness) thorough soakings per week should keep new plants thriving. Camellias in heavy soils or low areas where water puddles may deteriorate due to waterlogged conditions that promote root problems.

Fertilizing. Many theories and methods abound regarding camellia fertilization. Wintergarden recommends a fertilization schedule that has worked well for us. Our initial feeding is in early spring, after the camellias have flowered and new growth appears. In mid-July we fertilize a second time. Slow-release fertilizers with iron and trace minerals are much preferred. Avoid cheap, quick-release fertilizers. They may cause more harm than good. Water well prior to feeding. Fertilizing during dry conditions may result in injured plants. Be careful not to over-fertilize.

Disease. Camellias generally are strong plants that require little care if watered and fertilized properly. However, they are not problem-free. Along the Gulf Coast with its high humidity, fungal diseases such as root rot and stem dieback may occur. Annual soil drenches with a fungicide recommended by local garden centers should keep these problems under control. Flower blight, a fungus that attacks camellia blossoms, is a serious problem in some areas. This condition occurs only in flower tissue and does not affect the overall health of the plant.

Above: Camellia hybrid "Egas," hybrid of *C. japonica* and *sasanqua* combined best qualities of both species. Below: *Camella japonica* "Mrs. Walter Allan Variegated," a prolific bloomer even in cold winters.

Insects and Pests. Occasional pest control measures may be necessary to eliminate infestation or to ensure that healthy plants remain pest-free. The most common curse of camellias is scale—tiny insects that collect on the underside of leaves and ingest plant juices. Mites can also be a nuisance. Periodic inspection of plants will reveal if pests are present. Should spraying be necessary, consult a local garden center for a product that is effective in your area. Wintergarden uses and recommends Ultra-Fine oil spray, an environmentally safe insecticide.

Sun or Shade. Generally, camellias prefer a semi-shady area of filtered sunlight. There are varieties, particularly among the older japonicas, that can tolerate full sun, especially in a high-humidity climate. Typically, C. reticulatas and hybrids require some protection from the midday sun. As for blooms, white and pale pink-flowering plants usually perform better in a protected area. Tree cover may also benefit camellias during cold snaps.

Pruning. Pruning is necessary to shape camellias and to promote bushy growth. The best time for pruning is early spring when blooming is over. Additional cutting may be needed during the summer to remove old wood and unwanted shoots. Camellias

Above: *Camellia sasanqua* "Rose of Autumn," large, glowing flowers on an incredibly vigorous grower. Below: Camellia japonica "Tricolor Superba," an ancient variety with beautiful foliage and flowers.

should never be pruned after the end of June, because young bloom buds could be severed. At no time should camellias be sheared. Their beauty lies in their natural, graceful form.

Container-Grown Camellias. Some camellias develop bushy, stocky growth in containers while others such as Drama Girl and James Hyde Porter are tall and willowy.

While we prune our camellias on a regular basis, we recognize the distinction in growth between varieties and therefore do not "over prune" our plants. We believe our customers will be happiest with their camellias if they follow this rule of thumb.

Blossom Characteristics. Many wonderful variegated camellia flowers are multicolored due to a harmless virus con-

tained in the leaves and flowers. Certain varieties show this characteristic more than others. Often the leaves are mottled in yellow as well, a condition welcomed by some and disliked by others. Many gardeners merely prune any branches they feel contain too much yellow.

Biography: Bobby Green

Bobby Green is a landscape designer and owner of Green Nurseries in Fairhope, AL. He encourages the wide use of camellias by emphasizing their versatility in the garden. His grounds have become a repository for rare and endangered camellia cultivars salvaged from long-abandoned nurseries and gardens. He designed the Wintergarden at the Mobile Botanical Gardens.

Azalea

Azaleas for Mobile Bay

By Maarten van der Giessen

To truly understand the 'what' and 'why' of growing azaleas here on the Gulf Coast you really need a globe–you know, one of those Rand-McNally artifacts from your school days. Put your finger on Mobile Bay and gently spin the globe toward Africa. You'll cross the Sahara, travel a bit North of the Pyramids in Egypt, fly over the plains of Tibet. You'll visit Sichuan, Wuhan, and skirt to the South of Shang-Hi. Now we're coming to azalea country. Once we leave China's mainland we find ourselves sitting on the island of Yakushima in Kyushu, deep in the native range of Rhododendron kusianum and

R. sataense. It is from these we derive our magnificent 'Southern Indicas'. Yakushima is also several hundred miles south of the Kurume province that provides the azaleas that we've planted in profusion here for the past 100 years, and that suffer in our tropical summers. And this is my point: that to truly understand and successfully grow azaleas on the Gulf Coast, you need to understand what you mean when you say 'azalea.'

To tell the truth, it's not all that complicated. We can generalize a few things to the breaking point, and come up with a plan. You don't need to know every species of Rhododendron and it's native range to have healthy, happy azaleas. You do need to know four things; Indicas, Kurumes, Satsukis, and Encores. These four groups comprise the vast majority of the azaleas produced in the United

States, and differ from each other as radically as okra differs from hibiscus.

The traditional azalea of the Deep South is the Southern Indica. It adapts to Mobile like a cousin from Hattiesburg. Large foliage, large plants, early blooms, it is everything you think of when you say spring in Mobile. However, even these hardy plants need a little help to get established. We can start our 'How to Grow Azaleas' list with a few points, and these will apply to all the evergreen azaleas.

1. Avoid planting azaleas in full afternoon sun. Yes, I've seen the monster Formosa azaleas standing alone in the middle of the field, and yes with a little babying you can get the Indicas to live in our full, blazing sun (remember the Sahara?). But if you want to give yourself a break, azaleas always perform best under light, high shade.

2. Plant azaleas in soil rich in organic matter. Bill Finch, garden guru for the *Mobile Press Register*, plopped his directly into composted leaves heaped on top of the soil.

3. Azaleas need good drainage. This is not the plant for that soggy, dark spot in the back.

The Kurume azalea is perhaps the most misunderstood of our azaleas. It actually is a blend of *Rhododendron kiusianum*, *R. kaempferi*, and *R. sataense* that grow wild on Mount Kirishima near Kurume, Japan. Mount is the word to pay attention to here. The Kurumes are described as compact, medium sized azaleas, with masses of small, bright flowers. Take them to North Alabama and this is perfectly true. Put them in the sun here and they'll sweat like Yankees.

I used to hate Kurumes. Everywhere I looked well-meaning folks would set these out in front of their homes, and within a year or two they'd wish they'd never seen them. My friend Tommy Dodd said it best, "They're like Northern Women. The climate here won't kill them, but it sure makes them miserable." However, Bobby Green of Green Nurseries in Fairhope set me straight. It's not that they won't grow; it's how they grow. The Kurume azalea in Mobile is a graceful, open grower that is a magnificent addition to the woodland border. There are many variations in color and form that make this a special plant for the Southern palette. We'll add one more rule to the list we started: Be careful with the clippers. These girls are unforgiving. You can't prune these into gum balls and expect them to be happy about it.

The Satsuki group is the most popular azalea in Japan. If you

want to impress the girls, that's pronounced 'Saht-skee. If you want to be understood, pronounce it like it's spelled. It's a blend if *Rhododendron indicum* and *R. tamurae* from Yakushima (Remember where we washed up after our swim across the East China Sea?). Satsuki means 'fifth month' (based on the lunar calendar) in Japan, and indeed most Satsuki bloom here in late April and early May. The form of the plant is usually low, compact, and will respond well to a light shearing in June.

The flowers are almost impossible to describe. They vary from the Abstract Expressionist to the most delicate of Monet's Impressionism. The full range of possibilities is endless, and it was exactly that characteristic that captured the Japanese imagination. In the South, however, the Satsuki is little-known and hard to find. It's native range made it unsuitable for the population centers on the East Coast, and it has never been widely produced commercially. It is perfectly at home here. If you really want to see what azaleas can do on the Gulf Coast, then visit the Mobile Botanical Gardens in late April. They have the largest public collection in the South, and that Garden in full bloom is breathtaking. It's important to emphasize here that Satsuki need high shade. Without protection the flowers can suffer in our May summer heat.

So what about the Encores? Well, let's talk about what they are, and maybe we can understand how they work. The Encore Azaleas were developed by Robert (Buddy) Lee of Franklinton, Louisiana; one of the most respected azalea authorities in the United States. Buddy wanted an azalea that would re-bloom, so he mixed the three groups we talked about above with *Rhododendron oldhamii*, a brick-red, hairy, grouchy azalea from Taiwan that blooms profusely in September. The species is tender here, and needs some protection. Buddy knew this, and mixed his ugly friend with the tougher American hybrid groups. The results were varied and surprising. Virtually all of the Encores bloom profusely in the fall, perhaps less soin the spring, with a wide range of colors and forms. The Encores are well-suited for the deep South and represent a major accomplishment in American horticulture. That said—use caution. A garden full of Encore azaleas can be like a good tune whistled one too many times.

So what's the best azalea for your garden? All of them, of course. A mix of Indica, Kurume, Satsuki, and Encore can keep your garden in flower seven months out of the year. The joy of gardening is discovering diversity, and few groups celebrate that diversity better than the azaleas on Mobile Bay.

Biography: Maarten van der Giessen

Maarten van der Giessen attended the University of South Alabama. He was the assistant manager at Cottage Hill Nursery in Irvington, Al from 1987 to 1990 and has been manager and Vice-President of van der Giessen Nursery in Semmes, Al since 1990. He is a past president of the South Alabama Nurserymen's Association, a board member of the Azalea Society of America, and current president of the Mobile Botanical Gardens. Maarten has worked on the Aromi azalea hybrid group with Dr. Eugene Aromi since 1996, and has continued to evaluate and release Aromi seedlings after Dr. Aromi's death in 2004.

Amelia Rose.

Native
Azaleas

Native Azaleas

By Tom Dodd

Without getting too technical, let us define Native Azaleas as those deciduous members of the Genus Rhododendron that originated in our region before we got here and messed things up.

There are members of this group (all deciduous or losing their leaves in the winter) located from the Southern U.S. to the Northeastern U.S. and on the Left Coast. The three types found in L.A. are *Rhododendron canescens*, *R. serrulatum*, and *R. austrinum*. Most of the other types (or species) will also grow here, some better than others. Most of them prefer morning sun and afternoon shade as well as a well-drained site. They need water while getting established and planting in late fall is always a good idea.

The local populations of these three species are greatly diminished due to habitat loss and to a lesser extent, collection. They can still be seen during their bloom period in early spring in the woods on many of the local rural roads. They add light and fragrance to the area and are a wonderful addition to any garden.

Rhododendron canescens ("Piedmont Azalea" or Honeysuckle Azalea") varies in flower color in the wild from almost white to a medium pink. The flowers are tubular in shape and smell wonderful. They can mature to a height of 10 or 12 feet and usually bloom here in mid spring. There are many cultivated varieties in the trade now with different traits.

Rhododendron serrulatum ("Swamp Azalea") is white and usually, but not always, found near low areas. Different populations of this species bloom at different times of the summer, but most found in the trade bloom here in late June or early July and have a very pleasant fragrance.

Rhododendron austrinum ("Florida Flame Azalea") also varies in bloom color in the wild from a light yellow to a yellow/orange. The first cultivated variety of this plant was called 'Escatawpa', named for the river near where it was found. Many hybrids of this Azalea are now in the trade and range in color and bloom size all over the chart. This Azalea and her hybrids do better than most in our locale and can mature as low as 6 feet or as tall as 12 to 15 feet! The Confederate series of native azaleas are hybrids of R. *austrinum* and an Exbury type.

Other species that do well here include *Rhododendron alabamense*, R. *arborescens*, R. *prunifolium*, R. *flammeum* (old name is R. *speciosum*), R. *viscosum*, R. *oblongifolium*, and others.

R. *alabamense* ("Alabama Azalea") This azalea is white with a yellow blotch on the main ("Flag") petal. It is probably the most fragrant of all the species. It is found in the wild in the upper western part of our state.

R. *arborescens* ("Sweet Azalea") is found in the very upper eastern part of our state and blooms in the early summer. It is white with pink stamens and has a very pleasant fragrance. It will grow here in cool shade.

R. *prunifolium* ("Plumleaf Azalea") This azalea was made famous at Callaway Gardens over in Georgia. It blooms red or orange/red in the mid summer and is not fragrant.

R. *flammeum* ("Oconee Azalea") This species has almost every color you can imagine in the wild. It occurs over in Georgia and I have seen colonies that show pink, white, yellow, red or orange blooms. It isn't fragrant when it blooms in mid spring, but the colors almost make up for that shortcoming.

We have many of these Native Azaleas in our garden and get to enjoy various members bloom from late March until late summer. Most fill the air with a wonderful fragrance and make walking in the garden a real treat. We love to go out into the woods and see them in the wild but WE NEVER DIG THEM and people that do usually kill them. It is much better for all that we obtain them from a place that grows them commercially and doesn't harvest from the wild. If the site is to be destroyed, then it is best to move them in the winter.

There are pictures in many books of the various varieties and almost all of them can be found

Florida Flame Azalea, Rhododendron austrinum, has become rare in Alabama because of overcollection.

on the internet (get a teen-ager to look it up for you). Your local retail nurseries will have them during bloom time and you can visit and pick your colors. They are difficult to propagate, more expensive to produce, but are worth the extra expense.

When planting these native azaleas, we generally use a fertilizer that releases over a long period of time. These plants need minor elements as well so get a complete fertilizer and go very light with the dose. We use some of the Osmocote products but others with the same characteristics will work just as well. If you fertilize in the spring, use a 9-month granular type (liquid fertilizers last only a short while).

Everyone always asks about trimming these plants. I prefer to let them grow in a natural form as they will perform better and have fewer problems down the road. Just give them an area where they can grow and care for them until established (usually 1 year or so) and forget about trying to control something that doesn't need it.

For pictures of these plants, we invite you to look at our web site, www.doddnatives.com, and look in the part that says "Botanical Names" and the Native Azaleas head up the list.

You can scroll down, click on the picture and it will enlarge. You can even print the picture.

We encourage every gardener to have some of these beautiful plants in their garden to enjoy in the Spring and Summer.

Biography: Tom Dodd

Very Short Bio on Tom Dodd, III with all the bad stuff left out: Born in Mobile, Alabama on 5 March 1944 into a Nursery family (Tom Dodd, Jr. and Elizabeth P. Dodd). Attended Semmes School, grades 1-12. Attended The Citadel, 1962 thru 1966 - History Dept. Cross Country Team, Sailing Team. U.S. Army from 1967 thru 1971. Airborne school, Ranger school, Comanche County Cannon Cockers College. Viet Nam 1968 thru 1970 – 173 Airborne Brigade, 319th Artillery Forward Observer with 4/503rd Infantry, Battery Exec with D/319th Recon squad with 75th Rangers. Attended The Citadel 1971 thru 1973 -BS Biology. Attended College of Charleston 1973 thru 1974 - Marine Biology. Employed by Ciba-Giegy as a Chemist 1974 thru 1976. Employed by Tom Dodd Nurseries 1976 through 1988. Moved to Charleston to set up Nursery in 1988 with wife, Thayer, and watched it blow away in Hugo, 1989. Moved back to Mobile in 1991 with Thayer and started Dodd & Dodd Nursery and watched it get hammered by Ivan and then Katrina. (Still here doing native plants and other stuff). 4 children and 3.75 grandchildren. 4 Basset hounds, 1 Lab and several cats.

The fragrance of Honeysuckle Azalea, *Rhododendron canescens*, fills the air in early spring.

Florida Anise, *Illicium floridanum*, one of William Bartram's favorite plants

Native Plants

Mountain Laurel, *Kalmia latifolia*, one of the world's great landscape shrubs.

Let's Examine a Few Good Reasons to Use Native Plants.

By Fred Nation

Why should I use native plants in my landscape? This is a good question, and it deserves a thoughtful answer. Actually, there are several very good questions about choosing native plants for our yards and parks, and to enhance our roadsides. Let's examine a few of them.

Will it grow here?

For South Alabama native plants, the answer is "yes, and the evidence is all around us!" Our indigenous flora has been enduring and flourishing through thousands of long hot summers, droughts, and those vicious little "blue norther" cold snaps that freeze back our satsumas and early tomatoes. Natives are obviously well-adapted to conditions here in Lower Alabama, including our soils, which tend to be poor and acidic.

Where should I plant it?

For natives, we can often find the answer just by looking around! All plants are habitat-specific to some degree, and we can see where the different natives are growing in the wild. Generally, we can see that the showy flowering perennials, such as the sunflowers, like dry, sunny sites. Native azaleas are often seen in moist forests, in the

shade of larger shrubs and trees, and they will grow well with these conditions in the landscape. Many natives are pretty forgiving, within limits, to where they are planted. For example, most of our Iris species are found in marshes, but, with a little mulch and a little extra water, Iris do quite well as bedding plants in the landscape.

What care and maintenance does it require?

Any plant, native or exotic, will reward the care we give it.

Observation and simple common sense are good guides for care of our natives. For example, if your plants wilt, water them deeply, preferably in the morning. This is an important issue for newly installed landscapes. Woody landscape plants can be periodically pruned, but, fortunately, most natives look best when left to develop their own natural forms. Sparingly apply a slow-release fertilizer in early spring, and keep a couple of inches of mulch around your plants to buffer temperatures, discourage weeds, and hold soil

Our beautiful native Red Hibiscus, *Hibiscus coccineus*, is nearly extinct in Alabama.

moisture. In general, keep lime away from South Alabama Natives, which are adapted to well-drained, acidic soils. Soil tests are a great idea. Call your local Extension Office for information and to request a testing kit. The Extension Office is also a good place to seek expert help on the rare occasions when diseases or pests attack our plants.

Are native plants really good enough for landscapes?

When William Bartram traveled through what is today the Southeastern United States just before the American Revolution, he was here as a commercial plant collector! He was under contract to discover and collect plants of promise for the genteel gardens of Wealthy Englishmen. Some of the plants that Bartram admired and collected for his patron are still treasured and still widely grown today.

If natives are not good enough to stand on their own as trouble-free, attractive additions to our landscapes, no amount of cajoling will be enough to sell them. Are they good enough? The simple answer to this question is that some of the finest landscape plants that the world has to offer are native to the Central Gulf Coast of the United States. Here is a short annotated list of great South Alabama natives for the landscape.

Loblolly Bay, *Gordonia lasianthus.*
Loblolly Bay eventually becomes a large tree, but growth is so slow that it is treated as a small understory tree in landscapes, where it is sometimes used as an alternative to dogwoods. Gordonia is seldom more than 30 feet tall, with clean, evergreen foliage, and masses of

fragrant white, ruffled, three inch flowers that bloom from midsummer into fall. Loblolly Bay is a rare Alabama native that has become widely available in recent years from nurseries and plant sales.

Florida Anise, *Illicium floridanum.* Evergreen, aromatic foliage, with an upright habit, to 15 feet tall. Two inch   burgundy flowers in April; asterisk-shaped fruits lend multi-season interest. One of the world's great shrubs for moist, shady sites. 1775 Bartram wrote glowingly of the "groves of fragrant Illicium" in Baldwin County, Alabama.

Mountain Laurel, *Kalmia latifolia.* A big, robust, evergreen relative of azaleas and   blueberries. This southeastern native ranges from the Appalachian Mountains, south into Mobile and Baldwin Counties. Masses of beautiful five-sided pink or white flowers in spring have made Mountain Laurel one of the world's prized landscape shrubs for more than 200 years. It likes good light and a well-drained site with good moisture.

Stokes' Aster, *Stokesia laevis.* A spectacular herbaceous perennial, Stokesia was shipped to England and cultivated before 1770. It is easy to grow as a bedding plant in full sun, even in very poor soils. Three inch lavender flowers are show-stoppers in late spring.

Oakleaf Hydrangea, *Hydrangea quercifolia.* Our Alabama state wildflower, Oakleaf Hydrangea was discovered and named by William Bartram in 1775. It is a big deciduous shrub with large oak-like leaves, and masses of creamy white flowers in late spring. Red and orange fall foliage can be quite showy. Unlike nearly all gulf coast natives, this one likes a slightly basic soil pH, and responds well to a shovel-full of slag lime or oyster shells in the backfill when planting. Flowers are good in dried arrangements. Oakleaf Hydrangea is one of the great ones—a plant for all seasons.

Red Hibiscus, *Hibiscus coccineus.* We often select our   landscape plants to satisfy needs, such as to provide shade, to define space, or to mask unattractive structures. How about a great American native just for whimsy, because it is so beautiful? With brilliant red, six-to-eight inch flowers, Red Hibiscus will stop traffic in June and July. In the wild, it has become very rare in Alabama, but it is easy to grow as a large bedding plant, and can be purchased at garden centers and native plant sales. If you have a few extra feet of space in the flower bed, plant this one for your heart!

Stokes' Aster, *Stokesia laevis*, is an outstanding native perennial bedding plant.

Trees

Assessing, Selecting, Planting and Establishing Your Urban Forest

By Beau Brodbeck and Jack Rowe

In Alabama most communities are beginning to wake up to the fact that they have an aging urban forest. Look at most any community from Decatur to Mobile and you will see a profusion of old declining trees. Many of these trees were planted when these towns were founded over 100 years ago or were volunteer species (species that were not planted but became established naturally). Today the streets of Decatur and Mobile are beautifully, shaded, tree lined streets, but what about tomorrow?

Today in Alabama we have three major challenges. First, if we don't plant trees soon we may wake up one day to a tattered old urban forest with nothing to take its place. Second, we have a profusion of overly mature large trees that are increasingly beginning to pose a risk to our communities and need regular monitoring and care. Thirdly, we need to begin to plant trees well adapted to the environments where we expect them to grow.

We often plant tree species only because they are beautiful or fast growing. However, we need to be aware of the species we plant and how they will react to our environments. Along Alabama's gulf coast we have especially dramatic weather in the way of hurricanes. Planting species adapted to other regions may not have all the characteristics that make many of our native trees survive these hurricane force winds.

In this chapter my goal is to briefly outline three important compenents of arboriculture that every homeowner should apply to their yards. First and foremost "tree assessments", an important

Photo by KimPearson

process for inspecting existing trees for health and structure to determine if they present an acceptable level of risk. Second, "tree selection", an important component when considering both long and short term tree growth, survivability, and the potential risks these trees may pose in the future. Finally, tree maintenance, without proper maintanance we only spin our wheels for tree survivability decreases dramatically.

Identifying Weak Trees in Your Yard

Along the Gulf Coast we need to be a vigilant as possible because of our high wind environment caused by hurricanes. Trees failing during strong storms are a major source of property damage for the average homeowner. After all, what grows close by that shades your house/lawn/street and keeps you cool throughout the gulf coast summer?

Trees are amazingly long-lived plants, often large and heavy (those trunks and branches are all wood filled with water) and are a study in the physics of balancing forces. Substantial weights, pressures, and stresses are placed on roots, trunks, and limbs made of green wood. Homeowners along the gulf coast need to regularly inspect their urban trees for safety concerns to home and property. Identifying tree defects and figuring out what to do about it can be very difficult for someone unstudied in tree biology. Unlike most of

The first and best thing to understand about trees is that there is no such thing as a perfect tree. All trees will have various defects and/or decay that can lead to failure. Just living long enough to become a big tree usually means that trees accumulate problems, kind of like how we accumulate problems as we age; arthritis acting up anyone? The key is minimizing the risks and as Neil Letson, a forester with the Alabama Forestry Commission explains, "like any other valuable asset, better management increases returns and minimizes risks." In cities and suburbs most trees are street side or near a home or vehicle. Less risk equals less application for insurance payment or you having to pay for tree removal and major home.

The first step toward having safer trees is being proactive throughout the lives of your trees. As Letson explains there are three simple rules towards having safer trees—"systematic inspections, treating problems quickly, and removing a tree when its risks outweigh its value". Here along the Gulf Coast the risk of having unsafe trees with structural defects is especially problematic due to high winds generated by hurricanes.

To help you figure out if you have a problem that needs more careful checking by a professional, here are some important key signs that may give away a potentially weak tree. Always remember to examine every part of a tree, especially a large one; from all available angles and different distances to be sure you've looked at the WHOLE tree. The major parts to examine are the roots, the trunk, and the crown.

First, identify the tree species. Some species of trees are more susceptible to disease, decay, or structural problems than others. For example, water oaks, silver maples, and black cherries are fast growing and often become hollow, riddled with decay, and often structurally unsafe as they become mature.

After identifying the tree species begin by examining the roots. Root failure is one of the leading causes of a whole tree falling over during a storm. There are two primary types of root failure: first is soil failure, or soils that lose the ability to hold the root system in place. Such as saturated soils, which may be caused by overly aggressive watering or areas with poor soil drainage. Saturated soils when combined with high winds can lead to toppling trees and root failure. Look to see if your soil is continuously wet.

Secondly, there are root defects. While root defects may range from construction damage (roots got cut off) to limited growing space (not a lot of room to spread roots out) this article will focus on identifying root decay. Begin by looking for mushrooms or conks (toadstools or shelf fungus) growing on or near the base of the tree or on the ground under the tree. These growths are the fruiting bodies of decay and are signs of a serious problem within the tree. Decay can spread up the truck of the tree and down into the roots causing large hollows. If conks are seen contact a Certified Arborist to identify the extent of the decay within the tree to ensure the right management decision is reached.

Pay close attention to leaning trees, while a leaning tree doesn't necessarily mean it will fall, "it certainly warrants a closer look", explains Neil Letson. Leaning trees may have decay due to broken roots; if no conks are present a good indicator of a problematic leaning tree is a soil mound at the base of the tree on the opposite side of the lean. This is a common occurrence along Alabama's gulf coast due to hurricane winds. Leaning trees with mounding often

the other plants in your yard, trees are very complex and their problems often hidden from view or difficult to assess for health and structural integrity.

If you suspect a weak tree near your home, hiring a Certified Arborist is often the best decision. To become a Certified Arborist one has to pass an intensive exam covering 12 domains of arboricultural knowledge administered by the International Society of Arboriculture. This makes an ISA Certified Arborist a much safer choice for tree work and advice. Just ask when you call a company if the arborist that will visit you is certified by the International Society of Arboriculture. Certified Arborists will also feature their certification number or sticker on a truck, calling card, or paperwork.

the tree is unsafe. "The larger the size, the greater the risk", explains Letson. Additionally, the location of the decay such as near a junction of a large branch or near the base of the tree increases the risk. There are several signs of decay to look for in trees, which include mushrooms and conks, loose or missing bark, dead branch stubs still on the tree, cavities or hollows, carpenter ants or bees, nesting holes, oozing sap or fluids, and trunk bulges.

Decay within the tree trunk can lead to reduced capacity to withstand the pressured applied by tree weight combined with wind. If one of the above signs is identified quantifying the amount of decay is difficult and will require the use of specialized tools Certified Arborists can provide. Indicators of decay such as bulges, oozing holes, and carpenter ants are often all you may see from outside a tree. In assessing your trees it's important to realize that you may have to depend on these more obscure signs, because conks or mushrooms may not always be present.

Next examine the major branches of your tree. The same things you looked for on the trunk look for on the major branches with the addition of crotch angles. The angle at which the branch meets the trunk is extremely important in assessing how strong the attachment is. In general, but not always, a narrow angle means a weak point of attachment; a wider angle means a stronger attachment. The problem with narrow crotch angles is that the bark between the branch and the trunk interferes with how strongly the branch is attached to the tree. Weak attachments could cause branch loss during high winds.

indicates broken and damaged roots and should be examined by a professional immediately.

After a careful assessment of the roots it's time to move up the tree to the trunk and branches. Decay on trees results from some type of injury ranging from an old broken branch or pruning cut to some type of mechanical injury, such as a hitting a tree with a vehicle. Most trees will have decay or rotten wood somewhere on the trunk, the key is identifying whether it's impacting the trees structural integrity.

The size and location of the decay or cavity will determine if

The only tree part we haven't really looked at is the leaves/needles. These can really give you a great hint as to the overall health of the tree. Generally, lots of dark colored foliage well distributed over the whole canopy, and dense enough that seeing through the canopy is difficult, is good. If you see patchy foliage clustered together or if the leaves/needles are smaller and pale colored you should check the tree over again to see if you missed anything or call on a professional to check the tree for you.

This is a very casual inspection we've laid out here, intended to educate, not alarm. Living with trees means getting to know them well and treating them as the valuable assets they are. Inspect your trees regularly and protect them from undue harm and they'll reward you with home value, cool the local climate, and improve the quality of life for you and your neighbors.

Smart Growth in Urban Forestry; Using Hurricane Resistant Trees

Along Alabama Gulf Coast, where hurricanes are nearly a yearly occurrence, smart growth in urban forestry is important and residents of hurricane prone communities must consider planting hurricane resistant tree species to plan for future storm events. Planning an urban forest that matches the hurricane prone ecosystem is important. In the past there have been trends to plant non-native trees in our urban forests with low storm resistance. Previous fads like Bradford Pair (Pyrus calleryana) and non-native red and silver maples (*Acer rubrum and saccharinum*), once very popular, are now causing problems in communities as their low storm resistance causes these trees to break, split, and blow-over. The use of these low storm resistant species causes increased property damage, work for city urban foresters and personnel, and reduces the urban forest canopy cover. The need for careful tree selection to ensure trees with high resistance to hurricanes are planted is needed.

Research from the University of Florida and Auburn University

has developed lists of trees with high resistance to wind. These lists were developed by researchers visiting and sampling urban trees in communities impacted by hurricanes. Trees were assessed in urban neigborhoods for every major hurricane from Andrew in 1992 through Katrina and Rita in the summer of 2005. The results are a list of trees with high resistance to hurricanes, generally comprised of native tree species. Trees indigenous to coastal Alabama have developed in an ecosystem where frequent storms have enabled these trees to develop characteristics that allow them to survive in this hurricane environment.

Native trees species with wide spreading branches, small leaf size, low centers of gravity and planted in groupings seem to hold up better during storm events. Research has also indicated that slower growing trees generally have stronger wood characteristics that are more hurricane resistant than many of the faster growing trees with weaker wood fiber strength. So while it may take many of these tree species longer to grow, they will likely be around for many more years after a hurricane.

Increasing the use of these trees with a high resistance to hurricanes on city right-of-ways, in parks and on private yards will decrease damage and retain the green spaces within our communities. With fewer tree losses your community will recover faster and retain its urban forest, increasing the beauty and livability of you community while reducing work for yourself and your urban forester. Consider working with your local Extension agents, Urban Foresters, or City Horticulturalists to plant hurricane resistant trees to improve your urban forest's resistance to storms. Consider planting some of the following trees next time you look to replace a tree:

Small to Medium Sized Trees	Large Trees
Ironwood *Carpinus caroliniana*	Florida Sugar Maple *Acer saccharum subsp f.*
Redbud *Cercis canadensis*	River Birch *Betula nigra*
White Fringetree *Chionanthus virginicus*	Sweetbay Magnolia *Magnolia virginiana*
Dogwood *Cornus florida*	Southern Magnolia *Magnolia grandiflora*
Carolina Silverbell *Halesia tetraptera*	Black Tupelo *Nyssa sylvatica*
Chinese pistache *Pistacia chinensis*	White Ash *Fraxinus americana*
Goldenraintree *Koelreuteria paniculata*	Live Oak *Quercus virginiana*
Sand Live oak *Quercus geminata*	Bald Cypress *Taxodium distichum*
Chastetree *Vitex agnus castus*	Pond Cypress *Taxodium ascendens*
Saucer Magnolia *Magnolia soulangiana*	Schumard Oak *Quercus schumardii*
Japanese maple *Acer palmatum*	Swamp Chestnut *Qurecus michauxii*
Dahoon Holly *Ilex cassine*	White Oak *Quercus alba*
Yaupon holly *Ilex vomintoria*	Post Oak *Quercus stellata*
A. Hophornbean *Ostrya virginiana*	American Holly *Ilex opaca*
(Alabama Cooperative Extension System, Auburn University)	

Gearing Up for Tree Planting Season; Some Helpful Tips for Successful Tree Planting

Winter is considered the ideal season for tree planting in Alabama. Along the Gulf Coast the months between November and March normally provide the best climatic conditions for improved tree survival. During winter months, trees are dormant and transplanting shock is greatly reduced due to leaf fall and reduced photosynthesis and water requirements. However, successful tree planting goes beyond proper timing. It requires three major steps:

1. careful site evaluation
2. Proper planting techniques
3. Regular maintenance

Site evaluation:

Once you've decided to plant trees this winter, you're ready to evaluate the site. Homeowners should ask themselves the following questions when selecting a site for planting their trees.

1. Is irrigation available?
2. What is the light exposure, sun or shade?
3. What is the soil drainage?
4. What is the distance from the site to buildings?
5. Are there any overhead power lines?
6. Are there any below ground considerations, water, cable?

Answering these questions completely and honestly will be your first step to a successful tree planting project and will help you match the right tree to the right spot. However, regardless of the tree you select it is important that newly planted trees receive regular irrigation, especially during their first summer. Check to see if your site has a working irrigation system or if water source is available by hose or bucket. Current recommendations specify three gallons per "caliper inch" in diameter two to three times per week ("caliper inch" is measured six inches above ground level). Trees should be irrigated regularly during their "establishment period", and having easily accessible water will reduce your yard work ("establishment period" is about six months for each inch tree caliper thus a three inch tree has a eighteen month establishment period).

Another site feature important to tree selection is considering light exposure. Avoid planting trees that require lots of sunlight in shaded portions of your yard, and of course vice-versa. Simple research on the tree species you are considering or research on shade or sun tolerant trees will help you make a decision on where to place trees.

Additionally, it's important to consider your soil type and drainage. Planting trees requiring well drained soils, like Southern Magnolias on continuously wet sites will invariably cause that tree to grow poorly or die. It is important to evaluate your soil drainage. This is easily done by digging an eighteen inch hole and filling it with water, if after one to two hours the whole is empty you have good soil drainage and nothing to worry about. However, if after twenty-four hours the water remains, you have poor drainage and need to consider planting poor drainage tolerant species like Bald Cypress. (Note; if planting in well drained sites consisting primarily of sand consider sand tolerant species like Live Oak or Sand Live Oak)

When buildings and trees compete for space the consequences can be disastrous. It is very important in your site selection to avoid placing trees too close to buildings. Large tree species are often planted too close to buildings and in later years become nuisances or even hazards. Large trees species should be kept at least ten feet from homes to allow trees to develop full root systems more or less evenly distributed around the tree. If trees are planted too close to buildings, building foundations will often divert root growth laterally and cause trees to become unstable and more likely to blow over as they grow larger. This should be avoided, especially in hurricane zones such as the Alabama Gulf Coast.

Another important component to evaluating your site is remembering to "look up". Trees will invariably grow up and if they encounter power lines, only problems can result. Trees are either severely pruned or removed, because nobody likes losing their power due to falling limbs or trees. If you are looking to plant under power lines consider planting trees that grow less than thirty feet high like dogwood, Carolina silverbell, or crape myrtle. Larger trees should be kept at least twenty to thirty feet away from power lines.

Tree Installation:

Successful planting projects are very dependent on proper installation. The number one mistake made during installation is planting trees too deep. It is often assumed that roots have to be well below ground level. However, if planting containerized (trees grown in a container usually plastic) or ball and burlap (field grown trees dug and wrapped in wire and burlap to hold the roots in place) trees it is best to dig the hole too shallow rather than too deep.

Allow the rootball to be one to three inches above ground level. Additionally, do not loosen the soil below the tree but rather make the whole two to three times the diameter of the rootball to allow room for lateral root expansion (for example if the diameter of the container is twelve inches the hole should be thirty-six inches wide).

With the hole dug it's now ready for tree installation. Whether planting containerized or ball and burlap (B&B) you will need to remove either the container or at least the top three rungs of wire and all of the burlap, in the case of B&B trees, before installation. Leaving this material can greatly impact tree growth as roots develop. Additionally, in the case of containerized tree be sure to cut any circling roots that traverse more than half the distance around the container. If a tree has been in the container too long there will be a profusion of circling roots and the long term survivability of the tree will be greatly reduced, these trees should be returned if possible.

Finally, place the tree carefully in the hole and place the soil removed from the planting hole back in. Do not amend soils, this practice can cause circling roots and does not encourage trees to develop in a more widespread pattern. Using existing soils may slow growth at first but trees will be better established in the long term. (Note: Most trees do not require stacking, unless they are overly tall and in an area in your yard where regular wind can be a problem.)

Tree Maintenance:

Proper tree maintenance is the final component for successful tree planting. After the tree is installed place mulch two to three inches deep at least three feet around the tree. Do not pile the mulch around the tree's base, because this will keep the bark moist and increase the chances of unwanted insects and fungus. Most mulch commercially available will work adequately, such as pine straw, pine bark, or chipped wood. Trees should be re-mulched every year to keep competition down from grasses and other weeds.

Each planted tree will need care and maintenance to grow into a healthy specimen that can one day contribute to your yard and community. Below are some two important steps in maintaining newly planted trees which will improve survivability, strong tree structure, and tree health.

Year 1 Watering: Newly planted trees require 2-3 gallons of water for every inch in diameter (measured 6" above soil surface)

twice a week during the first one to three years depending on tree size. Watering helps young trees develop a root system that can sustain the tree and help it become established. The rule of thumb for tree establishment is six months for every inch in diameter. Note, the smaller the tree the faster it becomes established and thus the less watering it will require. Research has indicated that smaller trees are easier to establish and will often outgrow larger trees in a few short years (ideal landscape tree is 1"-2" in diameter).

Year 2 Pruning: "If a tree falls in the forest and no one is around does it make a sound?" In the rural forest this question may be valid, but in the urban forest you can bet on it. Unlike trees in a natural forest setting trees in the urban forest require regular pruning to ensure good structure. Good structure helps reduce the risk of tree failure by having solid branch attachments, no co-dominant stems or forks, and good branch distribution. Additionally, pruning trees when they are young will cause limited introduction of decay in cuts unlike pruning large or mature trees.

Broken limbs and split tops often equal property damage in the urban forest and the sounds or damage will not go unnoticed. To ensure a tree has good structure inspect the tree once per year and begin pruning after year two to remove:

1. Co-dominant stems or forks (forked trees often have included bark and are more likely to fail)

2. Problematic branches or branches that turn back into the tree or rub again other branches

3. Excess branches (you want branches evenly distributed up and around your tree. Too many branches in a single area will cause branches to be poorly connected to the main stem).

Biography: Beau Brodbeck

Beau Brodbeck was born and raised in Guatemala and moved to Alabama to pursue a bachelors of science in forestry from Auburn University. Upon completing his degree he worked for three years as a professional forestry consultant in Opelika, Alabama. In 2003 he returned to Auburn University to pursue a Master's of Science in forestry. Upon completion of his degree he took a position with the Alabama Cooperative Extension System managing the Hurricane Ivan and later Hurricane Katrina urban and community forestry grant programs awarded to Alabama in the aftermath of these storms. Additionally, Beau is an ISA Certified Arborist and an Alabama Registered Forester.

Container

Gardens

There Is Hardly Any Place More Suited to Container Gardening Than the Coastal South.

By Pat Libby

The long growing season; the climate, its variability and peculiarities; the architecture; the soil structure; its customs of entertaining guests; a general love of the outdoors; the number of retirees calling this area home, restricted mobility, and often more limited acreage; and a prevailing sense of creativity and spontaneity all combine to provide an environment most favorable to the use of containers for designing and creating gardens in pots.

There are many advantages to container gardening. Often the available soil is not well-suited to the types of plants the gardener wishes to grow; coastal soil is typically sandy or full of Alabama's famous red clay, a condition not conducive to growing hostas, spring bulbs, and a number of herbaceous perennials. It is also typically acid. Many plants need a larger dose of lime. Other plants need a longer exposure to cold temperatures. Tender plants can be grown outdoors in containers and moved inside when the weather becomes too chilly or too hot. Plant display is improved; trailing plants such as vinca, ivy, and creeping perennials have a chance to make a dramatic statement. Colors and textures can be combined or enhanced by the choices of height, size, and type of container and are unrestricted by nature. Eyesores can be hidden; bare or dull spots improved. There is less chance of pest damage, and, best of all, plants can be moved, to

show to their best advantage in whatever area the gardener chooses. Gone is the need for grids or garden plans, for this is a "moveable feast" for the eyes, if not also the stomach.

In choosing a container, the gardener needs first to consider the type of architecture of his home. A stately concrete urn would be no more suited to a log cabin than a painted tire to a plantation home. There are many choices, which include the lighter weight "look-alikes" for ceramic and clay pots; tin buckets and pitchers; wooden barrels; hypertufa; plastic growing bags. Should the gardener choose to use heavier natural materials or large containers, there are many forms of bases with casters to ease transportation. A large clay or ceramic pot filled with mature plants can be very heavy. Whatever placement, container type or size, the gardener is in control.

The next consideration is drainage, which is essential to the health of all plantings. Plants can "drown" from sitting in water as easily as they can become desiccated by the summer heat or lack of proper watering. If the container chosen does not have a drainage hole(s), onemust be drilled or other measures taken to ensure good drainage, such as coconut husk fiber, packing "peanuts," or even crushed recycled aluminum cans. Potshards are no longer

recommended for this; it is thought they might actually hinder drainage. What might be considered a disadvantage to container gardening is that the plantings must be watered more frequently than if they were planted in the ground, because more of the surface area (the container) surrounding them is exposed to the elements. Clay pots are particularly porous and absorb much of the water given plantings. They should be soaked before planting to give a good start and adequate moisture to new plantings.

When planting any container, the use of a limited amount of water-soluble crystals is an aid to retaining water available to the soil for longer periods, but is not a substitute for regular watering, especially in the coastal south. A drip pan or saucer is a must for proper drainage. First, it is an aid to the gardener to tell whether the pot has been filled, and, second, it keeps the drainage, often discolored (salts, minerals, soil particles) off the patio or path. There are some excellent and decorative "feet" for use under saucers to further aid in keeping the surface on which the planting is displayed clean and free of debris and mold, which often collects under a saucer placed directly on the surface. Mulch may be used on top of the soil, but it should be of a quality that does not "float" when the container planting is watered. Clustering plants gives them a little microclimate that will minimize moisture loss and increase humidity.

Planting the container is the product of the creativity of the gardener, who is both artist and landscape architect. He may choose his favorite plants or colors or color combinations, use a certain planting to lead the eye down a path or to a favorite garden sculpture or entrance, or attempt something new. If the prime consideration is continuous color, annuals should probably be considered, rather than one-time-blooming perennials, such as daylilies or amaryllis, which, though both well-suited to coastal gardening, once they have performed their annual bloom, may become unattractive as their foliage dies, or unwieldy as it grows. Annuals require careful attention to fertilization, and, remember, that annuals often re-seed themselves in this climate, so the gardener shouldn't be surprised if this year's plants pay a visit next year! A variety of colors, even if monochromatic, and textures adds more interest to the designer's creation. Considerations must be given to light exposure and to the fact that the usual last frost date for this area is February 28. Also, Baldwin County is considered mostly Zone 8 going into Zone 9 in the coastal area. Most plant labels include zonal information.

It is a good idea to plant something tall in the middle of the pot (or in back, if the pot is to be placed against a wall), also known as the "thriller"; something "bushy" or something with volume below that, also known as the "filler," surrounding the tall planting as transition material, and something to trail, the "spiller," on the edges. This combination is very satisfying to the eye. A good growing medium is important; these contain sterilized loam along with plant additives, such as peat, sand, bark chips, vermiculite, and perlite. Many are now available with several months' fertilizer incorporated into the potting mix. Potting soil should be placed so that, with the addition of the plants, it comes to within 1" of the top of the

container. In cases where this enhanced medium is not used, the incorporation of time-release pellets is encouraged. This does not take the place of regular fertilization, but is a boon to the growing plant and a bolster for the forgetful or absent gardener. One may also make his own potting soil mix from a number of available recipes. Soil from the yard or garden should not be used, as it may contain diseases or pests that might harm the fresh new planting or other nearby plantings. Any soil mix will become compacted over time, so, if containers seem waterlogged or heavy, plants seemingly in decline, the gardener may need to start afresh at the beginning of the next growing season or add a container booster mix, which recharges depleted soil. Always wear gloves when working with the soil, fertilizers, or pesticides. When choosing plants, it is always a good idea to take into consideration those that have similar light exposure, fertilizer, and water requirements. It would not do to plant succulents, which have a great tolerance for drought, with geraniums or verbenas, which require almost daily watering. One or the other would surely suffer.

The types of containers are almost endless, only as limited as the mind of the artist/gardener and the plant requirements. Free-standing pots may be home to a variety of plants or to one family or species, such as strawberry jars with their multiple openings for the trailing plants. Window boxes are a joy to those both indoors and out, and wall-mounted jars are appealing as a diversion from their earthbound cousins. Hanging baskets are present in one of every three gardens and can hold specific plants, or a variety, so long as they share common requirements. These particularly need more frequent attention to watering, because they are not only subject to more surface exposure, but to wind as well. There are many types of hanging baskets, from solid to wire lined with husks. The gardener must determine what type would work best for his choice of plant

and its destination in the landscape. There are also towers, which are basically some type of wire or plastic bag affixed to a wall; growing bags, which are usually horizontal and suitable for bulbs; converted, which include wheelbarrows, wire shaped basket containers, old buckets, boats, tree stumps, tires, even old crank ice cream freezers; raised beds; and cachepots (anything that will hold an existing planted pot and which can provide the necessary drainage.) And who can resist the call of a cool pond or fountain lushly planted on a warm summer day!

Container grown plants are relatively pest-free, since they have been so carefully and hygienically placed, but the coastal south does have its share of hungry varmints, such as deer, rabbits, and other "night-bloomers" who are not shy about sampling your fare. These and the plantings subject to certain known pests can be handled by a visit to a good nursery and a thorough reading of the labels on pesticides recommended for your particular problem. If you are uncertain about the problem, it is always wise to consult the Home and Gardens Infoline maintained by Agricultural Extension Service-trained Baldwin and Mobile County Master Gardeners who use only research-based material in their problem-solving.

Container gardens depend on their creator for fertilization. Fertilization is determined by the type of plant used and its ease of use by the gardener. Usually, a well-balanced water-soluble fertilizer, such as 10-10-10, used every two weeks is adequate for non-blooming or sparsely blooming plants, whereas one with a higher middle number, representing phosphorus, which regulates bloom quality and quantity is more suited to blooming plants, also used every two weeks during the growing season. A few plants, such as bougainvillea, are heavy feeders and may require weekly feeding. If one has container plantings that are trans-seasonal, fertilization can be spread out to once a month or less, perhaps increasing or

decreasing the time span if the plant blooms at a certain time, and depending on the needs of the plant.

Before even beginning planting, the gardener has certainly already selected a site. Containers of beautiful flowers or greenery say "Welcome" at the front door or gate to the patio. A spectacular container with an equally spectacular planting can be a focal point for the garden though containers should not compete with the floral display for attention. Containers can line a patio or terrace, create a path, "march" up the steps to a portico, reach welcoming "hands" down from a balcony or rooftop, enhance a bare windowsill or wall. Container plants can temporarily hide a bare spot or unsightly view. Once the display is faded or the event is over, the plants may be easily moved back to their original location or to a new one, and routine maintenance, such as "deadheading", pruning, supplemental planting or replanting can take place.

Almost every southern home has a "room" outdoors—a patio, terrace, a "secret garden," an entry way, or balcony. Such a room can be achieved by the use of planted containers even if there are no architectural boundaries just by maneuvering the choice of plants and containers, height, and size of both, or the use of trellises, pergolas, arches, and gazebos to produce privacy, a gathering area, a welcoming area, an entertainment area. It can be colorful and exciting, or a place of rest and relaxation, all determined by the gardener/designer. A plant list of horticulture known to do well in coastal southern container plantings is included at the end of this chapter, but it is by no means intended to name all cultural species that are available or recommended. The gardener needs to read a few books on the subject and peruse the home and garden magazines for ideas, and then produce a container garden of his dreams the likes of which have been in existence since pre-biblical times.

PLANTS SUITABLE FOR CONTAINER GARDENING
(This is by no means a COMPLETE list, rather a guide to get started)

TREES
Pine (pinus species)
Hinoki false cypress (Chamaecyparis obtusa cultivars)
Cut-leaved sumac (Rhus typhina 'Dissecta')
Crape Myrtle (Lagerstroemia indica)
Harry Lauder's Walking Stick (Corylus Avellana 'Contorta')
Japanese Maple (Acer palmatum)
Weeping Yaupon holly (Ilex vomitoria 'Pendula')
Bonsai

BEDDING PLANTS
Periwinkle (Vinca Minor)
Impatiens
Begonia
Petunia
Verbena
Bougainvillea spectalis
Geranium (pelargonium)
Angelonia
Pentas

Dusty Miller (Senecio cineraria)

VINES and TRAILERS
Greater periwinkle (Vinca major)
Ivy (Hedera Helix)
Creeping Jennie (Lysimachia nummularia)
Chenille (Acalypha hispida)
Asparagus "fern" (Asparagus densiflorus
'Springerii')

HARDY PERENNIALS
Cacti and Succulents
Canna (Canna xgeneralis)
Lantana species
Pitcher Plants (Sarracenia spp.)
Crinum lily (Crinum americanum)
Umbrella plant (Cyperus alternifolia)
Cast iron plant (Aspidistra elatior)

BULBS
Some daffodils, tulips, crocus

ROSES
Heritage roses
Some hybrid teas
China
noisettes

VEGETABLES
Tomatoes
Some beans
Squash

HERBS

FRUIT
Melons
Citrus

AQUATIC PLANTS
(for water gardens in containers)

Biography: Patricia Libby

Patricia Libby is a native of North Carolina, a graduate of Duke University in Art History, a Master Flower Show Judge for over thirty years, and a Master Gardener, having begun this study in her   previous home in AR and again in Baldwin County upon retiring to Foley, AL with her husband, Peter. The Libbys have lived in six southern states and have two children and two grandchildren.

Pat has numerous interests as well as gardening, and is currently participating as a volunteer patrol for the Share the Beach program, saving sea turtles on the Gulf Coast. She is an avid reader, an enthusiastic walker, a lover of cooking, and an occasional artist. These interests —and gardening—have led her to volunteer positions with the Gulf Shores Garden Club, the Garden Club of Alabama, the Garden Club of Alabama Council of Flower Show Judges, the Foley Public Library, the South Baldwin Newcomers, and the Baldwin County Master Gardeners. She loves the beach, and, in her spare time, she keeps house!

Water
Gardens

Native Plants for Water Gardens

By Fred Nation

Water gardens are hot! These interesting landscape features have been constructed in large numbers throughout South Alabama. They are often called "backyard ponds," but this name does not do justice to such wonderful additions to the landscape. Far from simply holes dug in the ground, water gardens are carefully planned and intensively landscaped. They are great examples of the magic of landscape architecture: planning, building, nurturing and carefully managing an area to create the illusion of small, pristine natural habitats. Water gardens also offer great opportunities to showcase rare or spectacular native shrubs, such as Witch Alder, *Fothergilla major*, or Fringetree,

Chionanthus virginicus, in peripheral areas adjacent to the pond.

Since ponds are so popular, it follows that the nursery trade has responded to the ever-increasing demand for aquatic and emergent plants. Many nurseries and garden centers now offer plants for ponds, and a few even specialize in plants, equipment and supplies for water gardeners.

Many aquatic plants, including some spectacular ones, are exotic; they have been imported and propagated for sale from all over the world. Exotic plants are by no means undesirable simply because they are exotic, but, unfortunately, a few have demonstrated the potential to escape cultivation and become invasive, causing great harm to our natural habitats.

The most famous aquatic invasive exotic is probably Water Hyacinth, *Eichornia crassipes*, a beautiful South American species that has

Pickerelweed, *Eichornia crassipes*.

and Eurasian Watermilfoil are now quarantined by the Alabama Department of Agriculture's new Noxious Weed Rules, which prohibit their transport into or within Alabama.

Here's some good news: Weeks Bay Reserve has constructed a water garden at the Interpretive Center, near Fairhope. Native aquatic and emergent plants have been selected exclusively, to make a strong case that our native species can be used to construct educational and visually spectacular water gardens. As it develops, this demonstration project will become an invaluable resource for water gardeners. We will be able to see first-hand the sizes, growth rates and general desirability of various

choked lakes, ponds and waterways throughout the South. Others include Eurasian Watermilfoil, *Myriophyllum spicatum*, Water Lettuce, *Pistia stratioides*, and Water Clover, *Marsilea sp* (several species). Water Lettuce

natives. Sources for native aquatic plants will also be determined and shared as they become available.

Here is a short list of just a few of the native plants that have been suggested for the Weeks Bay Water Garden. These plants can be added to the pond in their pots. Weighted down and concealed by a few rocks, they can be changed-out and replaced by others as often as you like.

↗ Pickerelweed, *Pontederia cordata*.

Clean, lanceolate foliage, with pretty blue-purple summer flower spikes.

↗ Fragrant Waterlily, *Nymphaea odorata*.

Large white or pinkish flowers, with clasic "lily pad" leaves. Surely one of the world's most beautiful wildflowers.

↗ Blue Flag Iris, *Iris virginica*.

Iris have spectacular color when in bloom, and clean, interesting foliage through most of the year.

➤ River Oats, *Chasmanthium latifolium*.

A dramatic, shade tolerant native grass that likes wet feet. Related to and looks similar to Sea Oats, though smaller. A good choice for the marginal areas around ponds.

➤ Lizard's Tail, *Saururus cernuus*.

Heart-shaped leaves. Spikes of white flowers in late spring-early summer. Shade-tolerant.

➤ Duck Potato, *Sagittaria* sp.

Several species. *S. latifolia* has arrowhead-shaped leaves and curious white flowers on a tall stem.

➤ American Lotus, *Nelumbo lutea*.

This one grows large, with big buds that open into spectacular creamy yellow flowers. One or two will add an interesting vertical dimension to the water garden. The receptacles, containing the round seeds, are often sold for dried arrangements.

➤ Swamp Lily, *Crinum americanum*.

Also called "Seven Sisters." Large, showy white flowers in mid-late summer.

A final word: be sure to properly dispose of plants that are removed from the water garden. Composting is the best way to deal with plant refuse—especially the exotics. And be sure to consider our beautiful native flora for any landscape setting, including the marginal areas around the water garden.

Garden
Accents

Garden Accents Add So Much to a Garden.

By Jim Priest

When placed properly, they can add texture where only soft plants are, interest where none exist and a punch of color where the backdrop is mostly green. They can also carry your eye to an otherwise unnoticed area of the garden. Water feature accents such as fountains can add the benefit of sound to the pleasure of the garden. Corners and angles are softened with the addition of accents such as pottery or statuary. Even the monotony of a hedgerow can be broken with a well-placed accent.

By simply placing a bench in the garden, it adds an inviting

touch; but when positioned as a focal point with other items such as planters or pottery, it can become an entire sitting area. Place a bird-bath in the garden and it adds interest, but with ornate feeders and decorative statuary or features it can become a bird garden. Putting a vintage wrought iron gate between two shrubs, creating the illusion of an old fence line, can create a simple but decorative barrier. And there is no better way to make a courtyard or patio look finished than groupings of planters or pottery placed along the edges and corners.

Accent lighting is an accent that is often under-used. It works in just about every garden or landscape by changing a humdrum garden scene by day into a totally different visual interest of shadows by night. For impact and value there is nothing that has the punch it provides. Let me be clear though, I am not talking about the cheap

and inexpensive packaged lighting that some people inadvertently and mistakenly use to replicate an airport runway along their drive. I am talking about good quality metal and glass accents and well placed up lighting, usually very tasteful with an obvious quality and durability to them. With   proper accent lighting, live oak trees now take on a new surreal effect, river birch trees go from common to dramatic when the sun goes down and an illuminated pathway is very inviting while adding an additional benefit of safety.

Choosing the right item for your garden is a   simple as finding what makes you happy, but it can also be a showcase when planned

carefully. First you decide which direction and style you want to go in. Is the home and landscape traditional or contemporary? Do you want to keep the look throughout the garden or do you want to take a different direction completely? My experience is that the style of the home is enhanced if there is a flow of design from home to landscape to garden. If your home is French country then old world pottery and stone accents work very well. Even formal cast iron urns can work, but folk art would have to be carefully   scrutinized so that no kitsch ruins the theme. Remember the wood cutouts of white ducks with blue bows or the image of the woman bent over in her garden?

Sometimes cute has a short shelf life however, timeless pieces like topiary forms in quality pottery or urns can last a lifetime or be passed down.

There are exceptions to the "rule of flow" such as Japanese gardens, English gardens and country gardens, which work well in most any style of home and can rarely match the rest of the landscape. If you should choose to go with the Japanese garden theme, accents of bamboo or stone is a must. An occasional Japanese lantern or Buda statue would certainly set the tone.

English gardens are mainly floral affairs but birdbaths and statues with a mild formality will keep the objective clear. Iron urns and topiary forms will also get the point across. This is another garden that you would want to avoid kitschy folk art.

Then there are the country gardens where you can use folk art to your heart's content: birdhouses, old wooden chairs, statuary or animals, old bed headboard and frames for a "flowerbed" and worn screen doors. But like the English garden, keep the flowers the dominant element.

There are types of accents for all types of gardens where they are used in moderation to give a personal touch to a grouping of plants. Which brings me to the phenomenon of the "Happy Yard"! You've seen them with Greek statues surrounded by little red capped gnomes, whirly gigs, "precious moment" eyed animals, and of course, folk art, all strewn throughout the landscape with what would appear as chaos. It isn't though; the owner chose each item because it makes them happy and it was placed in the yard for the same reason. After all, isn't that the purpose of a garden...to give you a sense of pleasure and happiness?

Accents of pottery, stone and iron give personality and character to every garden and landscape. With a little imagination, you can transform a good landscape into an enjoyable, interesting or happy escape right outside your back door.

Biography: James (Jim) E. Preast

James (Jim) E. Preast owns a small retail nursery in Fairhope. He also works closely with a landscape company he was instrumental in founding. From 1998 to 2005 he worked for one of the largest growers in the southeast, McCorkle Nurseries, working primarily in sales. Jim is certified in the state of Georgia as a "Nurseryman" or "Green Industry Professional" license #475. He assisted Rick Pierce in founding Planting Solutions Inc. a landscape and irrigation company, as a hands-on consultant who procured materials, customers, contacts and methods. In his career, Jim has operated two separate retail garden centers, done landscape installation, landscape design (in Georgia) and maintenance with a medium sized company, and was briefly a groundskeeper.

His father had a small landscape and growing operation when Jim was a youth, which introduced him to the plant industry.

by Stacy Howell

The Art and Beauty of the Garden.

Lagniappe

by Stacy Howell

by B Summerall.

by Christine Linson

Basket and Two Vases by Mary Ann Nelson.

by Christine Linson

White Flower in a Tall Vase *by Suzanne S. Wright*

Painting by Emily Lyons

by B Summerall.

by Christine Linson

Zinnias in a Gold Bowl by Dorotha Mattox

by Shan McClain

Gebera Daisy by Ron Thompson

Cosmos and Cobalt by Betsy B. Adams

The Good Earth *by Missy G. Patrick*

Dad's Koi Pond *by Kellie Lowe*

Girl in Greenhouse *by Christina*

In The Garden *by Jolane Edwards*

Hummingbird *by Susie Bolton*

Modern Flowers *by Jeanne Ruff*

The Montrose Post Office *by Christine Linson*

Retreat *by Stacy Howell*

Straw Burro from Segovia *by Kay Godshalk*

The Flower Girls
by Benita Hatfield

Fairhope fire hydrant

by Stacy Howell

by Anna Hood

by Emily Lyons

Part Three

Resources

Plant-a-pedia

A

Acuba *Acuba japonica*

African Daisy *Arctotis stoechadifolia*

African Iris *Arctotis*

Agapanthus *Agapanthus fricanus*

Ageratum *Ageratum houstonianum*

Alabama Azalea *Rhododren alabamense*

Alamanda *Alamanda cathartica*

Althea, Rose of Sharon *Hibiscus syriscus*

Amaryllis *Hippeastrum hybrids*

American Holly *Ilex opaca*

American Lotus *Nelumbo lutea*

Anise *Illicium floridanum*

Arrowhead *Sagittaria*

Ash *Fraximus*

Asparagus *Asparagus officinalis*

Asparagus Fern *Asparagus densiflorus*

Aspidistra, Cast Iron Plant *Aspidistra eliator*

Autumn Fern *Dropteris erythrosora*

Azalea *Rhodendron*

B

Baby's Breath *Spirea Spirea thunbergii*

Banana Shrub *Michelio figo or Michelia skinneriana*

Baldcypress *Taxodium distichum*

Basil *Ocimum basilicum*

Bay *Laurus nobilis*

Beach Morning Glory *Ipomoea imperati*

Beach Panic Grass *Panicum amarum*

Beach Sunflower *Helianthus debilis*

Beans *Phaseolus sp.*

Bear-grass *Xerophyllum tenax*

Bee Blossom *Gaura lindheimeri*

Beets *Beta sp.*

Begonia/Hardy Begonia *Begonia grandis*

Blackberry *Rubus*

Blackberry Lily *Belamcanda chinensis*

Black-eye Susan *Rudbeckia hirta*

Black Tupelo *Nyssa sylvatica*

Blanket Flower *Gaillardia pulchellos*

Blood Sage *Salvia coccinea*

Blueberry *Vaccinium ashei*

Blue Flag Iris *Iris versicolor*

Boston Fern *Nephrolepsis exaltata*

Bottlebrush *Callistemom citrinus*

Bougainvilla *Bougainvillea*

Boxwood/English Boxwood *Buxus sempervirens*

Bradford Pear *Pyrus calletryana*

Bromeliad *Aechmea fasciata*

Burford Holly *Ilex cornuta*

Bushy Bluestem *Andropogon glomeratus*

Butterfly Bush *Buddleia davidii*

Butterfly Ginger *Hedychium coronum*

C

Cabbage *Brassica sp.*

Cabbage Palm *Sabal palmetto*

Caladiums *Caladium x hortulanum*

Calendula *Calendula officinalis*

Calla Lily *Zantedeschi sp.*

Camellia *Camellia japonica*

Camellia Sasanqua *Camellia sasanqua*

Canna Lily *Canna x generalis*

Cardinal Flower *Lobelia cardinalis*

Cardinal Shrub *Weigela*

Carissa Holly *Ilex cornuta*

Carolina Yellow Jessamine *Gelsemium sempervirens*

Carolina Silverbell *Halesia tetraptera*

Cast Iron Plant *Espedistra elatior*

Catbriars *Smilax*

Celeus *Celeus x hybridus*

Centipede Grass *Eremochloa ophuiroides*

Century Plant *Agave Americana*

Chastetree *Vitex agnus*

Chinese Evergreen *Aglaonema sp.*

Chinese Pistache *Pistacia chinensis*

Chinese Wisteria *Wisteria sinensis*

Chives *Allium schoenoprasum*

Chrysanthemum *Chrysanthemum sp.*

Citrus

Clematis *Clematis hybrids*

Cleome *Cleome hassleriana*

Cleyera *Ternstroemia gymnanthera*

Cockscomb *Celiosa argentia*

Coleus *Solenstemon scutellarioides*

Collards

Coneflower Purple *Echinacea purpuria*

Confederate Jasmine *Trachelospermum jasmenaides*

Confederate Rose *Hibiscus mutabilis*

Coral Berry *Ardisia crenata*

Coreopsis *Coreopsis sp.*

Corn *Zea mays*

Cornflower *Centaurea cyanus*

Cosmos *Cosmos sp*

Crape-Myrtle *Lagerstroemia indica.*

Creeping Juniper *Juniperus horizontalis*

Crocus *Crocus sp.*

Cucumber *Cucumis*

D

Daffodils and Narcissus Early Types *Narcissus sp.*

Dahlia *Dahlia hybrids*

Dahoon Holly *Ilex cassine*

Daylilies *Hemerocallis hybrids*

Delphinium *Conslida ajacis*

Dianthus *Dianthus hybrids*

Dill *Anethum graveolens*

Dogwood/Flowering Dogwood *Cornus florida*

Dusty Miller *Senicio cineraria*

Dutch Iris *Xiphium hybrids*

Dwarf Southern Magnolia
Magnolia grandiflora 'Little Gem'

E

Eastern Red Cedar Tree *Juniperus virgiana*

Eggplant *Solanum melongena*

Elaegnus *Eleagnus pungens*

Elephant's Ear *Alocasia*

English Boxwood *Buxus sempervirens*

English Ivy *Parthencissus tricuspidata*

Euonymus *Euonymus japonicus*

European Fan Palm *Champerops humills*

F

Fennel *Foeniculum*

Fern *Seleginella martensii*

Fig *Ficus carica*

Fig Vine *Ficus pumila*

Flag Iris *Iris pseuydacorus*

Flame Azalea *Rhododendron calenduloceum*

Florida Anise *Illicium floridanum*

Florida Flame Azalea *Rhododendron austrinum*

Florida Sugar Maple *Acer saccharum subsp.*

Flowering Kale *Brassica oleracea*

Flowering Quince *Chaenomeles speciosa*

Flowing Tobacco *Nicotiana*
Forsythia *Forsythia X intermedia*
Foxglove *Digitalis purpurea*
Fringe Tree *Chionanthus virginious*

G
Gardenia *Gardenia jasminoides*
Golden Rain Tree *Koelreuteria paniculata*
Dwarf Gardenia *Dwarf gardenea radicans*
Gaura *Gaura lindheimeri*
Geranium *Geranium sp.*
Gerbera Daisy *Gerbera jamesoni*
Ginger *Zingiber*
Ginger Lily *Hediphium coronarium*
Ginkgo *Ginkgo biloba*
Gladiolus *Gladiolus sp.*
Gourds *Lagenaria, luffa or cucrbita sp.*
Grancy Greybeard *Chionanthus viginicus*

H
Hardy Begonia *Begonia grandis ssp. evansiana*
Hibiscus/Rose of Sharon *Hibiscus syriacus*
Hickory/Shellbark *Carya ovata*
Holly *Ilex sp.*
Holly Fern *Cyrtomium falcatiom*
Honeysuckle Azalea *Rhododendron canescens*
Honeysuckle, Major Wheeler *Lonicera sempervirens*
Hosta *Hosta sp.*
Hydrangea *Hydrangea sp.*
    Hydrangea macrophylla
    Hydrangea macrophylla marissa
    Hydrangea serrata 'Blue Bird'

I
Impatiens *Impatians wallerana*
Indian Hawthorne *Raphiolepisis indica*
Iris *Iris sp.*
Iris *Iris pseudocorus*
Ironwood *Carpinus caroliniana*
Ivy *Hedera helix*

J
Japan Cleyera *Ternestromia gymnanthera*
Japanese Black Pine *Pinus thunbergii*
Japanese Cryptomeria *Cryptomeria japonica*
Japanese Holly *Chromium falcate*

Japanese Magnolia *Magnolia soulangiana*
Japanese Maple *Acer palmatum*
Japanese Painted Fern *Athyrium nipponicum pictum*
Japanese Wisteria *Wisteria floribunda*
Juniper *Juniperus sp.*

L
Lady Bank's Rose *Rosa banksiae*
Lady Fern *Athyrium filix – femina*
Lantana *Lantana sp.*
Leatherleaf Mahonia *Mahonia bealei*
Lettuce *Lactuca sativa*
Lilac Chaste Tree *Vitex agnus-cactus*
Ligustrum *Ligustrum japonicum*
Lily *Lilium sp.*
Liriope, Bigblue *Lariope muscore*
Live Oak *Quercus virgiana*
Lobelia *Lobelia x sp.*
Longleaf Pine Tree *Pinus palustris*
Loropetalum *Loropetalum chinense*
Louisiana Iris *Iris fulva*

M
Maidenhair Fern *Adiantum pedatum*
Magnolia *Magnolia grandiflora*
Mandevilla *Mandevilla sanderi*
Maple *Acer*
Marigold *Tagetes hybrids*
Melapodium *Melapodium paludosum*
Mint *Mentha sp.*
Mondo Grass *Ophiopogon japonicus 'nanus'*
Moss Rose *Portulaca grandiflora*
Mother-In-Law's Tongue *Sansevieria trifasciata*
Muhly Grass *Muhlenbergia capillaris*
Muscodine Grape *Vitis rotundifolia*

N
Nandina *Nandina domestica*
Narcissus *Narcissus*
Nasturtium *Tropaeolum*
Native Azalea *Rhodendron sp.*
Needle Palm *Rhapidophylum hystrix*
Nun's Orchid *Phaius grandifolius*

O
Oakleaf Hydrangea *Hydrangea quercefolia*

Oconee Axalea *Rhodendron flammeum*
Okra *Abelmosochus esculentus*
Oleander *Nerium oleander*
Onion *Allium cepa*
Oregano *Origanum sp.*
Ornamental *Kale or Cabbage*
Osmanthus *Osmanthus fragrans*
Oxeye Daisy *Chrysanthemum lucanthemem*

P
Pansy *Viola*
Parsley *Petroselimem crispum*
Peace Lily *Spathiphyllum sp.*
Pear *Pyrus*
Peas *Pisum*
Pecan *Carya illinoensis*
Pentas *Pentas lanceolata*
Pepper *Cassicum annum*
Periwinkle *Vinca minor*
Persimmon *Diospyrous virgiana*
Petunia *Petunia hybrida*
Pickerel Weeds *Scabious columbaria*
Pinecone Ginger *Zingiber zerumlet*
Pincushion flowers *Scabiosa*
Pine Tree *Pinus sp.*
Pittosporum *Pittosporum tobira*
Pitcher Plant *Nepenthes*
Plum *Prunus x domestica*
Plum Leaf Azalea *Rhodondron prunifolium*
Pomegranate *Punica granata*
Pond Cypress *Taxodium ascendens*
Poppy *Papaver*
Post Oak *Quercus stellata*
Potato *Solano tuberosum*
Primrose *Primula*
Privet, Japanese *Ligustrum japonicum*

R
Rain Lily *Zephyranthes sp.*
Redbud *Cercis Canadensis*
Red Maple *Acer rubrum*
Red Oak *Quercus rubia*
River Birch *Betula nigra*
Roses *Rosa*
Rosemary *Rosemarinus prostrates*

S

Sage *Salvia officinalis*
Sage Palm *Cycas revolute*
Salvia *Salvia sp.*
Sand Live Oak *Quercus geminata*
Sasanqua Camellia *Camellia sasanqua*
Saucer Magnolia *Magnolia x souliangiana*
Saw palmetto *Serenoa*
Schumard Oak *Quercus schumardii*
Schefflera *Brassaia actinophylla*
Scotch Ivy *Araliaceae*
Sea Oats *Uniola paniculata*
Sea Oxeye Daisy *Borricchia frutescens*
Sea Perslane *Ssusuvium portulaca castrum*
Sedum *Sedum sp.*
Seaside Goldenrod *Solidago sempervirens*
Shasta Daisy *Chrysanthum x Superbum*
Shore Juniper *Juniperus conferta*
Siberian Iris *Iris sibirica*
Snap Bean *Snapdragon antirrhum*
Southern Bayberry *Myrica pensylvanica*
Southern Maiden *Adiantum caoillus*
Southern Magnolia *Magnolia grandiflora*
Spider Lily *Hymenocallic latifolia*
Spinach *Spinacia*
Spirea *Spiraea sp.*
Split-Leaf Philodendron *Phildendron bipimanalifidum*

Squash *Curcurbita*
Star Jasimine *Trachelospermum jasminoides*
Star Magnolia *Magnolia stellata*
St. Augustine Grass *Stenotaphrum secundatum*
Stock *Matthiola*
Stoke's Aster *Stokesia cyanea*
Strawberry *Fragaria*
Sundew *Drosera*
Sunflower *Helianthus annus*
Swamp Azalea *Rhodenron serrlatum*
Swamp Chestnut *Quercus michauyii*
Sweet Alyssum *Lobularia maritrimo*
Sweet Azalea *Rhododendron arborescens*
Sweetbay Magnolia *Magnolia virginiana*
Sweet Olive *Osmanthus fragrans*
Sweet Pea *Lathyrus latifolius*

T

Taiwan Cherry *Pruness campanulata*
Thrift *Pllemon iaceae*
Thyme *Thymus vulgaris.*
Tickseed *Coreopsis grandiflora*
Tomato *Lycoperiscon*
Treasure Flower *Gazania hybrida*
Trumpet Vine *Campsis tagliabauna*
Tupelo *Nyssa*
Turnip *Brassica rapa*

U

Umbrella Plant *Cyperus alterniflius*

V

Verbena *Verbena sp.*
Vinca/Periwinkle *Vinca minor*

W

Walking Iris *Neomarica northiana*
Wax Begonia **Begonia semperflorens-cultorum**
Wax Myrtle *Myrica cerifera*
White Ash *Fraxinus Americana*
White Fringetree *Chionanthus virginicus*
White Ginger Lily *Hedychium coronarium*
White Oak *Quercus alba*
Wild Rosemary *Eriocephalus africanus*
Windmill Palm *Trachycarpas fortunei*
Wisteria/Chinese Wisteria *Wisteria sinesis*

Y

Yarrow *Achilles sp.*
Yaupon Holly *Ilex vomintoria*
Yellow – Flag Iris *Iris pseudocorus*

Z

Zinnia *Zinnia elegans*

Importance of Soil Testing

By Monte L. Nesbitt, Horticulturist, Auburn University

Plant growth and vigor is dependent on having an adequate amount of sunlight, water, proper surface and internal drainage of water, and soil chemical factors suitable to the species of plant. The latter is assessed through soil sampling. Taking a soil sample is recommended when planning to introduce new plants into the garden or landscape, or when identifying a possible plant nutrient disorder or deficiency. Soil samples identify existing levels of major and minor essential levels as well as the soil pH reaction, which determines nutrient availability.

Soils along the Gulf Coast in Alabama vary considerably in their physical texture and chemistry, with sandy soils near the water and clayey soils found inland. It is common to find that heavier textured soils (loams, clays) in our area are acidic, with a pH around 5.0. Azaleas, camellias, and blueberries are examples of plants that prefer low pH soils, but many others will grow better when the pH is raised by the addition of lime to 6.0 or higher. The only way to know whether the pH is suitable for the plants being grown is by collecting a soil sample and having it analyzed by a soil testing lab.

Soil texture (sand versus clay) similarly affects how many essential nutrients are present in the soil. Sandy soils have poor retention of nutrients (nitrogen, phosphorus, etc.), and thus require more frequent applications of fertilizer and at higher rates. Again, soil sampling from the area of the landscape where plants will be grown is the only way to know how much and how often fertilizer should be applied.

Soil assessment in Alabama is done for a nominal fee by the Soil Testing Laboratory, located at the main campus of Auburn University. The procedures for how to collect and prepare a sample, as well as mailing procedures are found at the website: www.aces.edu/pubs/docs/A/ANR-0006-A/. There are two approaches to sampling. When troubleshooting problem areas of the landscape, collect samples from immediately around the problem plants. If the same species of plant is performing well in one location but poorly in another, two distinct samples from each location provides the best way to solve whether the problem is really a soil nutrient problem. Composite samples (collecting and combining from multiple sites) are good for assessing the "average" fertilizer and liming requirements for lawns or vegetable gardens where horticultural practices will be uniform.

Retail Sponsors

You may purchase additional copies of *In Full Bloom* at the store locations of the following retail sponsors. The Montrose Garden Club is grateful to these retailers for their support of this important project.

Old Tyme Feed and Garden Supply
Cecil Christenberry
www.oldtymefeed.com
251-928-1156

Preast's Petals & Pottery
Jim Preast
8263 Gayfer Avenue Ext.
251-928-6073 email: rjpreast@yahoo.com

Page and Palette
Karin Wilson
32 South Section Street, Fairhope, AL 36532
251-928-5295 email: Karin@pagenadpalette.com
www.pageandpalette.com

Clementine, Inc
Hubert and Lark Fleury
410 Fairhope Avenue, Fairhope, AL 36532
251-928-5755 email: fleuryfair@aol.com

Stagecoach Café
Joyce Overstreet
52860 State Highway 59, Stockton, AL 36579
251-580-0608

Grand Hotel Marriott® Resort Gift Shop
One Grand Boulevard
P.O. Box 639, Point Clear, AL 36564
Phone: 1-251-928-9201 www.marriottgrand.com
Elizabeth's Garden
250 McGregor Ave. North,
Mobile, AL 36608
251-344-2654

Bellingrath Gardens and Homes Gift Shop
12401 Bellingrath Gardens Road
Theodore, AL 36582
www.bellingrath.org
1-800-247-8420

Zimlich's Patio & Garden Center, Inc.
2650 Dauphin Street
Mobile, AL 36606
251-478-1484
www.zimlichspatio.com

Section Street Gallery of Fine Art
58 South Section Street, Fairhope, AL 36532
"Fine Gift and Investment Art"
Benita Hatfield McNider
251-928-6933 benitaart@bellsouth.net

Nelson Galleries
56 South Section Street, Fairhope, AL 36532
"Art, Antiques, Gifts"
John Edward Nelson
251-928-6933

Springhill Medical Center Gift Shop
3719 Dauphin Street,
Mobile, AL 36608
251-344-9630

Eastern Shore Centre
30500 State Hwy 181 Suite 310
Spanish Fort, Al 36527
Vince and Lynn Boothe
Hagan Anderson and Teal Creel
251-626-7225
objectso@bellsouth.net

Resources

Louise Estes
Westminster Village
500 Spanish Fort Blvd, Spanish Fort, Al 36527
www.estesart.com
251 626-4106

Image Art
Brian Kasch
www.iaphoto,net; 251 421-9100

Fairie Tale Orchids
Virginia Boehme 251 605-7028

Kim Pearson
wwwkimpearsonphotographs.com
kimiark@aol.com; 251-490-9393

Stephen Savage
www.savagepictures.com
savagephoto@msn.com; 251 401-0008

Alabama Cooperative Extension System
Baldwin County 251 937-7176
Mobile County 251 574 8445

The Montrose Garden Club
PO Box 583, Montrose, Alabama 36559

Master Gardner Helpline/Southwest Alabama
February 1 to November 15
Baldwin County- Monday, Tuesday, Wednesday
Mobile County- Thursday, Friday
10 am to 4 pm; 1-877-252-4769

Baldwin County Master Gardener Plant Sale
held in March at Weeks Bay
Weeks Bay Plant Sale held the second weekend in October

Mobile Botanical Garden Plant Sales are held in the spring and fall.
www.mobilebotanicalgardens.org
251 342-0555

Bellingrath Gardens and Homes
12401 Bellingrath Gardens Road
Theodore, Al 36582
wwwbellingrath.org
Bellingrath@bellingrath.org;
1 800-247-8420 or 251 973-2217

Hem Haven Nurseries Daylilies
20205 Lawrence Road, Fairhope, AL 36532
John and Nancy Falck
251- 928-3340
www.edaylilies.com

Patrons

The Montrose Garden Club gratefully
acknowledges these Patrons who have made
the publishing of In Full Bloom a reality.

Dr. and Mrs. Rodger L. Grissett

Jan Ruffin/World Travel

John and Rosemary Hart

John and Bea Sheldon

Silverhill Kids Park

Jack and Lois Boykin

Valrrie V Faddis

Helen Gwin and Jack Nelson

Elizabeth Rockwell

James and Dorothy Bodiford

J. Martin and Norma Pitts

"Happiness is a shovel under my foot."

—Virginia Boehme